BIO
DIVERSITY

EXPLORE THE DIVERSITY OF LIFE ON EARTH

WITH ENVIRONMENTAL SCIENCE ACTIVITIES FOR KIDS

Laura Perdew

Illustrated by Tom Casteel

Titles in the **Environmental Science** book set

Check out more titles at www.nomadpress.net

Nomad Press
A division of Nomad Communications
10 9 8 7 6 5 4 3 2 1

This book was manufactured by CGB Printers,
North Mankato, Minnesota, United States
March 2019, Job #265269

ISBN Softcover: 978-1-61930-751-3
ISBN Hardcover: 978-1-61930-748-3

Educational Consultant, Marla Conn

Questions regarding the ordering of this book should be addressed to
Nomad Press
2456 Christian St.
White River Junction, VT 05001
www.nomadpress.net

Contents

Interested in Primary Sources?

Look for this icon. Use a smartphone or tablet app to scan the QR code and explore more! Photos are also primary sources because a photograph takes a picture at the moment something happens.

You can find a list of URLs on the Resources page. If the QR code doesn't work, try searching the internet with the Keyword Prompts to find other helpful sources.

🔎 biodiversity

GEOLOGIC TIME SCALE

WORDS TO KNOW

geologic time: the span of Earth's history marked by major events and changes.

era: a division of geologic time.

period: a division of time within an era.

epoch: a division of time within a period.

The timeline of Earth's lifespan is shown in a **geologic time** scale. It is broken up into chunks of time called **eras**. Each era is made up of different **periods**. Some of the more recent periods are also divided into **epochs**.

MILLIONS OF YEARS AGO

4,600			541.0	485.4	443.4	419.2	358.9	323.2
			Paleozoic					
Precambrian			Cambrian	Ordovician	Silurian	Devonian	Mississippian	Pennsylvanian
			Age of Marine Invertebrates			Age of Fishes	Age of Amphibians	

Origin of life

Early bacteria and algae

Simple multicelled organisms

Complex multicelled organisms

Early shelled organisms

Rise of corals

Trilobite maximum

Primitive fish

First land plants

First forests (evergreens)

First amphibians

First reptiles

Sharks abundant

Coal-forming swamps

MASS EXTINCTION

MASS EXTINCTION

FORMATION OF EARTH

GEOLOGIC TIME SCALE

This geologic time scale includes important events in Earth's history. Some of these events include the appearance and disappearance of different species, major changes in the earth that have caused mass extinctions, and how the planet has changed.

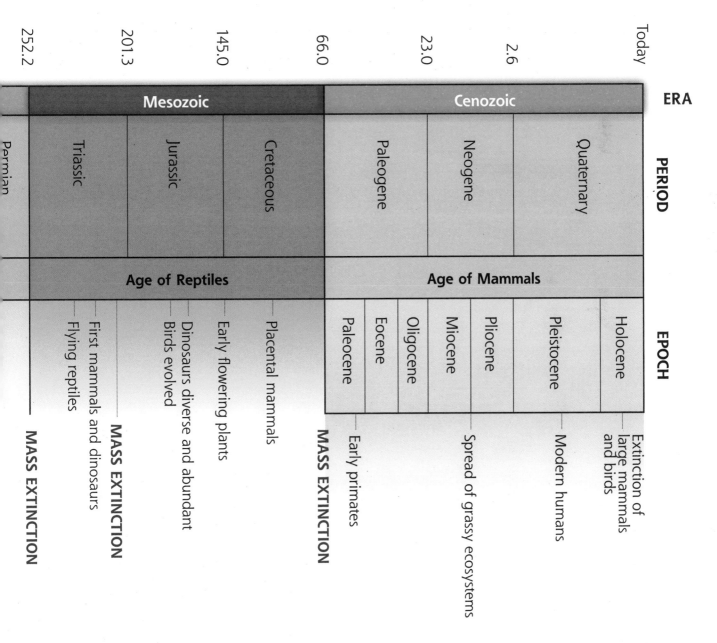

WHAT IS
BIODIVERSITY?

Step outside and take a look around. What kinds of creatures do you see? Any insects flying through the air? Any dogs, cats, birds? What about flowers and other plants? Don't forget the organisms you can't see—there are plenty of living species that are visible only with microscopes.

Humans share the earth with millions of other species. Millions! This variety of life on Earth is called **biodiversity**. Biodiversity includes plants, animals, **fungi**, **bacteria**, and **microorganisms** of all shapes and sizes. Biodiversity includes you! It also refers to large species such as blue whales and polar bears and giant redwood trees. There are medium-sized species such as saguaro cacti, wolves, and dolphins, as well as small species—ladybugs and tree frogs and forget-me-not flowers.

ESSENTIAL QUESTION

How is everything on the planet related to everything else?

WORDS TO KNOW

organism: a living plant, animal, or single-celled form of life.

species: a group of living things that are closely related and can produce offspring.

biodiversity: diversity is a range of different things. Biodiversity is the variety of life on Earth.

fungi: the plural of fungus, an organism that has no leaves, flowers, or roots and that lives on dead or rotting organic matter. Mushrooms are a fungus.

bacteria: microorganisms found in soil, water, plants, and animals that are often beneficial but sometimes harmful.

microorganism: a living thing so small that it can be seen only with a microscope.

ecosystem: an interdependent community of living and nonliving things and their environment.

biotic: of or relating to living things.

abiotic: of or relating to nonliving things such as temperature, wind, precipitation, soil type, and more.

kelp: a tall, brown seaweed that grows in forests in shallow ocean waters close to shore.

This National Geographic video is a photographic introduction to the wonders of the amazing biodiversity on Earth. **Check it out!**

🔍 Nat Geo biodiversity video

Biodiversity includes organisms so small they can be seen only with a microscope! In fact, in every square foot there are hundreds, sometimes thousands, of species growing, squirming, wiggling, flying, multiplying, eating, and thriving.

Why is this important? Why do we care that there are so many different species, especially when we can't even see them?

Polar bears are part of our biodiverse world!

INTERCONNECTED ECOSYSTEMS

All life on Earth is interconnected. Organisms, together with their physical environment, form a community called an **ecosystem**. Within an ecosystem, both the **biotic** and **abiotic**—or living and nonliving—factors work together to maintain the balance of nature. If one part of the ecosystem changes or disappears, the whole system is out of balance. People call this the web of life because if one connection breaks, the whole web may be affected.

The web of life is like a well-tuned machine. All the biotic and abiotic factors are the nuts, bolts, and gears that each play a role in keeping the machine in good working order.

For example, along the shorelines of California, sea otters eat sea urchins. Sea urchins eat giant **kelp**. When the number of sea otters drops, the number of sea urchins rises. All those sea urchins then destroy the giant kelp forests.

Kelp forests are also affected by changes in water temperature, light, and pollution.

A giant kelp forest
credit: Clinton Bauder (CC BY 2.0)

WORDS TO KNOW

erosion: the gradual wearing away of the earth's surface, usually by water or wind.

carbon dioxide (CO₂): a colorless, odorless gas. Humans and animals exhale this gas while plants absorb it—it is also a by-product of burning fossil fuels.

atmosphere: the mixture of gases that surround a planet.

Without the kelp forests, dozens of species that rely on the kelp for survival are at risk. Kelp helps protect shorelines from **erosion** and absorbs **carbon dioxide (CO₂)** from the **atmosphere**.

Kelp forests are just one ecosystem. Other large ecosystems include deserts, forests, grasslands, wetlands, jungles, and oceans.

Ecosystems can also be small, such as a cave or pond or tide pool, or even microscopic, including the ecosystem that exists under a rock. The parts within a single ecosystem are interconnected, and all the world's ecosystems are connected to each other.

They are like pieces of a puzzle that make up planet Earth.

DID YOU KNOW?

John Muir (1838–1914), an American naturalist, author, and environmentalist, once commented, "Whenever we try to pick out anything by itself, we find it hitched to everything else in the universe."

SO IMAGINE THIS IS AN ECOSYSTEM.

HOW ABOUT A GIANT KELP FOREST?

PERFECT!

IF EACH OF THESE PIECES ARE PART OF THE ECOSYSTEM...

...LIKE THE NUMBER OF OTTERS OR SEA URCHINS,

WHAT HAPPENS WHEN WE TAKE A PIECE OUT OF THE ECOSYSTEM?

BOOM!

I GET IT! THE WHOLE THING COLLAPSES.

This fungus is growing on a tree. Take a magnifying glass outside to look at a tree. What do you see on the bark? On the leaves?

LIFE ON A TREE

To better understand biodiversity and how ecosystems are interconnected, let's take a look at a tree. The tree itself is a living organism. What else lives there? A bird, maybe. Perhaps a squirrel. In some parts of the world, there might be a monkey or a sloth up there. Look closer. Is there a vine growing on the tree? There could be moss, too, or some other type of plant. Fungi can also grow on trees.

Look even closer! You might spot insects on the bark, such as ladybugs, aphids, spiders, caterpillars, or beetles. And, most likely, there are insects under the bark, too.

WORDS TO KNOW

boreal forest: a forest of coniferous trees found in the cold temperatures of the Northern Hemisphere.

genetic diversity: the variety of genes within a species.

gene: instructions within cells that affect how an organism will look, grow, and act.

cell: the smallest unit, or building block, of an organism.

adapt: to make changes to survive in new or different conditions.

species diversity: the variety of species living in an area.

mammal: an animal that has a constant body temperature and is mostly covered with hair or fur. Humans, dogs, horses, and mice are mammals.

current: the steady flow of water or air in one direction.

equator: an imaginary line around the earth, halfway between the North and South Poles.

theory of evolution: a scientific theory that explains how species change through time and how all species have evolved from simple life forms.

DID YOU KNOW?

The largest organism on Earth is a fungus! This giant underground fungus covers almost 4 square miles of land in the Blue Mountains of Oregon.

There is also life in and on the tree that you can't see. Bacteria, both helpful and harmful types, often grow in trees. There are many other microorganisms within the tree, all hidden from our sight.

There are an estimated 3 trillion trees on the planet. Not only are trees home to a huge number of species, they also give us oxygen, food, and shelter. They reduce the pollution in the air. Their roots help to hold soil in place. They provide shade on hot summer days. And, especially important today, they pull carbon dioxide out of the atmosphere.

Each tree is a miniature ecosystem for the species that depend on it and the tree is also part of a larger ecosystem, such as a rainforest or **boreal forest**. Trees play an important role in the overall health of the earth.

LEVELS OF BIODIVERSITY

Scientists study biodiversity on three levels: genetic, species, and ecosystem.

Genetic diversity is the variety of **genes** found within a species. Genes are the traits passed from parents to their offspring that affect behavior and looks. They are the instructions for the **cells** in an organism about how to grow and work. Your own genes were handed down to you from your biological parents. These genes determined your eye color, your height, and more.

Take dogs as an example. Some are large, some are small, some have floppy ears, others have pointy ears that stick up from their heads. There are hound dogs, retrievers, cattle dogs, lap dogs, guide dogs, and guard dogs. They all belong to the same species—dog. But the differences in behavior and appearance is because of the genetic diversity within the species.

When looking at biodiversity in an area, genetic diversity refers to the variety of genes in a population. And, the more genetic diversity there is, the more likely species will be able to **adapt** to changing environments. That's because some individuals will have traits that make them better able to handle changes and fight off new diseases.

> So, even when things change in an environment, genetic diversity allows some individuals of the species to survive.

Species diversity is the number of different species in an area. This includes plants, animals, fungi, bacteria, and microorganisms. Coral reef ecosystems have great species diversity. They are sometimes called the rainforests of the sea because of the amount of species diversity. Within a reef ecosystem, there are thousands of species of plants and animals, including fish, crabs, eels, turtles, sharks, shrimp, sponges, marine **mammals**, and more. These species interact with each other and the environment.

Galápagos Islands

The Galápagos Islands lie more than 600 miles off the west coast of Ecuador, in the Pacific Ocean. This area sits where three ocean **currents** meet and it straddles the **equator**. Because of this location and isolation, the collection of 19 islands is well-known for its biodiversity, much of which is found nowhere else in the world. The English naturalist Charles Darwin (1809–1882) visited the islands during a round-the-world tour in 1835. It was on the islands that Darwin developed his **theory of evolution**.

BIODIVERSITY

Scientists have named and recorded approximately 2 million different species on Earth. But, there are millions of species out there that have not yet been discovered! Scientists don't agree on the total number of species on Earth, but they estimate that there are between 2 million and 12 million. Some studies have even suggested that there could be a trillion species sharing the planet with us!

Within an ecosystem, species diversity contributes to the overall stability of the ecosystem. In other words, as species diversity increases, so does the health of the ecosystem. This also means that the ecosystem will be better able to handle changes within it.

Ecosystem diversity is the variety of ecosystems, **habitats**, and biological communities that exist in an area. This includes both biotic and abiotic factors. One important thing to keep in mind is that ecosystems come in all sizes. They also don't have definite borders. Therefore, different ecosystems are interrelated, so the loss of one ecosystem and the species within it will affect other ecosystems around it.

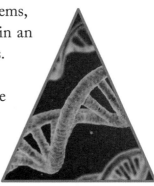

Genetic

The greater the ecosystem diversity in an area, the healthier the entire area will be, and the better able it is to adapt to changes in the environment.

To keep the levels of biodiversity straight, think of it this way: genetic diversity is the variety of genes within a species, species diversity is the variety of species within an ecosystem, and ecosystem diversity is the variety of ecosystems within an area.

Species

Ecosystem

In *Biodiversity*, you'll learn more about these three different types of biodiversity and what they all have to do with you, a human! You'll discover some of the ways that biodiversity on Earth is threatened and what every individual can do to help protect the amazing variety of organisms that share our planet. Let's go!

DID YOU KNOW?

Biodiversity is not evenly distributed among ecosystems. Colder ecosystems tend to have less species diversity than warmer ones.

Good Science Practices

Every good scientist keeps a science journal!

Scientists use the scientific method to keep their experiments organized. Choose a notebook to use as your science journal. As you read through this book and do the activities, keep track of your observations and record each step in a scientific method worksheet, like the one shown here.

Question: What are we trying to find out? What problem are we trying to solve?
Research: What is already known about the problem?
Hypothesis/Prediction: What do we think the answer will be?
Equipment: What supplies are we using?
Method: What procedure are we following?
Results: What happened? Why?

Each chapter of this book begins with an essential question to help guide your exploration of biodiversity and the environment. Keep the question in your mind as you read the chapter. At the end of each chapter, use your science journal to record your thoughts and answers.

ESSENTIAL QUESTION

How is everything on the planet related to everything else?

DISCOVER THE THREE LEVELS OF BIODIVERSITY

The three levels of biodiversity are all around you. Take a closer look and find samples in a nearby ecosystem! Use your senses to see, hear, smell, and touch the variety of life around you.

> **Caution:** Do not taste anything you find outdoors unless you have an expert adult with you who can identify it as something safe to eat!

> **Take a walk near your home or school.** After you've been out for a while, find a spot to comfortably sit.

> **Start by observing the genetic diversity around you.** Pick one species to observe, without touching. If you are in a forest, you might look at a stand of ponderosa pine trees, a family of ducks, or a group of mushrooms. How are the individuals different from one another? In your science journal, record how the different individuals of the same species look and act differently. This is genetic diversity.

> **Now look further.** How many different species can you see from where you are sitting? Record everything you notice. If you are on a beach, you might see different types of beach grass, shore birds, and sand crabs. This is species diversity.

> **Finally, can you identify ecosystem diversity from where you sit?** In the forest, that itself is an ecosystem. But there may also be a rotting log that is its own ecosystem, or a stream or pond. At the shore, there are ecosystems both in the water and on land. There may also be tide pools that are their own ecosystems.

Consider This

How might your observations change in a nearby natural area or different season? How about in an entirely different area? Each time you visit a natural area, take the time to observe what you see. Try to identify the levels of biodiversity there.

Chapter 1

A SHORT HISTORY OF
LIFE ON EARTH

Imagine a sea of bubbling lava. That's what the whole surface of the earth was like when the planet formed 4.6 billion years ago—just molten, bubbly rock. When the planet formed, the temperature of the earth's surface was more than 2,000 degrees Fahrenheit (1,094 degrees Celsius). There was no oxygen. No water. And there certainly was no life on Earth. In fact, it took 800 million years just for the planet to cool enough that the earth's crust became solid!

ESSENTIAL QUESTION

How has life on Earth become so diverse?

Then, roughly 3.6 billion years ago, the first life on Earth emerged—simple, tiny organisms that consisted of just one cell. Those very first single-cell organisms survived on a planet covered by a shallow sea.

WORDS TO KNOW

molten: turned into liquid through heat.

anaerobic: able to live without oxygen.

evolve: to gradually develop and change over time.

cyanobacteria: a type of aquatic bacteria that produces oxygen through photosynthesis.

aquatic: related to water.

photosynthesis: the process plants use to turn sunlight, carbon dioxide, and water into food.

gravity: the force that pulls objects together and holds you on Earth.

Great Oxygenation Event: the introduction of oxygen into the earth's atmosphere more than 2 billion years ago.

invertebrate: an animal without a backbone.

Bizarre Biodiversity

Narwhal: These marine creatures are the unicorns of the sea. This species of whale lives in the Arctic.

It was a harsh environment. The atmosphere had a lot of carbon dioxide and almost no oxygen. But those single-celled organisms didn't need oxygen to survive—they were **anaerobic**.

From those very first single-celled organisms, new organisms evolved. Biodiversity increased.

Cyanobacteria were one of the new life forms. These **aquatic** organisms were different because they used the sun's energy for **photosynthesis**. In the process, they produced oxygen as waste.

How Did the Earth Form, Anyway?

Before our planet took shape, a gigantic cloud of dust, rocks, and gas was swirling in space. As time passed, **gravity** drew these particles together. As more and more objects joined the mass, it grew and grew. A good way to think about this is to think of a snowball. To make one, you bring together many, many snowflakes. You are the gravity. As you add snow, the snowball gets bigger. Soon you have formed a perfect snowball. In the case of Earth, our planet formed.

Jellyfish have been on Earth for more than 500 million years.

Those tiny organisms were responsible for the build-up of oxygen in our air during the course of millions of years! This **Great Oxygenation Event** took place approximately 2 billion years ago.

About the same time, organisms with more than one cell emerged. While those first multi-cellular organisms were still quite simple, they gradually became more and more complex. About 600 million years ago, the complex, multi-cellular organisms were the beginnings of simple plants and animals. Earth's first animals were **invertebrates**, such as jellyfish, worms, and sea sponges. At this point, all life on Earth was still in the ocean.

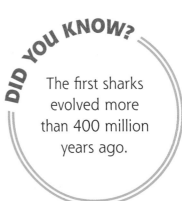

DID YOU KNOW?

The first sharks evolved more than 400 million years ago.

WORDS TO KNOW

hydrothermal vent: a fissure in the sea floor where super-heated fluid comes out.

mineral: a naturally occurring solid found in rocks and in the ground.

appendage: a part of an animal or plant that sticks out from the main part it is attached to, such as an arm or leg.

trilobite: an ancient arthropod that lived during the Paleozoic era.

arthropod: an invertebrate animal with a segmented body and limbs with joints, such as a spider or insect.

PALEOZOIC ERA

The timeline of major events on Earth is shown on a geologic time scale. It marks major changes in the earth's structure as well as the time when species both appeared and disappeared. The timeline is broken into chunks of time called eras. Each one of these eras includes different periods. And some of the recent periods are further divided into epochs. Look in the front of this book to see a chart of the different time segments on the geologic time scale.

DID YOU KNOW?

Scientists have identified more than 20,000 different types of trilobites.

The Precambrian time was the first 4 billion years of Earth's lifetime.

How Did Life Begin?

We know that life on Earth started with simple, single-celled organisms. But how did that first life begin? No one knows for sure, but there are several theories. One theory suggests that life formed at the bottom of the ocean near **hydrothermal vents**, which contained all the right ingredients and conditions to start life. Another theory proposes that the first life on Earth was actually a hitchhiker from somewhere else in space! According to this theory, life arrived on our planet on a meteorite or asteroid. Finally, a third theory says life started with a lightning bolt. The electricity in a lightning bolt, under the right circumstances and with the right chemical and **mineral** ingredients, might have helped to create the building blocks for life. Scientists are still working to solve one of the greatest mysteries of our planet.

That was when the first life appeared on Earth and oxygen built up in the earth's atmosphere. But it was during the first period of the Paleozoic era that life on Earth really diversified.

Named after the period in which it happened, that diversification was called the Cambrian Explosion. During this period, roughly 545 to 495 million years ago, underwater life thrived. Life on Earth began to resemble something out of a Dr. Seuss book!

This was the first time that life on Earth had bodies with heads, tails, and **appendages** such as fins, tentacles, antennae, and limbs. Giant, shrimp-like creatures were up to 6 feet long. An Opabinia was a small, five-eyed creature with a long, trunk-like nose.

Trilobites were ancient **arthropods** that looked like a cross between a scorpion, horseshoe crab, and turtle. They lived in the water and ranged in size from less than a half inch long to 2 feet! Trilobites also had eyes and a hard shell—two features that were new to the animal world.

A trilobite fossil

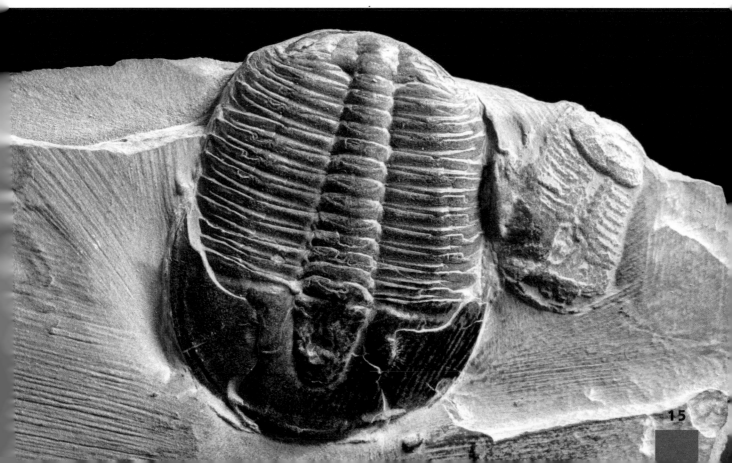

WORDS TO KNOW

vertebrate: an organism with a backbone or spinal column.

evolution: the process by which species change through time.

reptile: an animal covered with scales that crawls on its belly or on short legs. A reptile changes its body temperature by moving to warmer or cooler places. Snakes, turtles, lizards, alligators, and crocodiles are reptiles.

amphibian: an animal with moist skin that is born in water but lives on land. An amphibian changes its body temperature by moving to warmer or cooler places. Frogs, toads, newts, efts, and salamanders are amphibians.

mass extinction: a period in the earth's history when very large numbers of species die out in a short period of time.

tsunami: an enormous wave formed by a disturbance under the water, such as an earthquake or volcano.

ejecta: materials thrown out, as from the impact of an asteroid.

climate: average weather patterns in an area during a period of many years.

extinction: the death of an entire species so that it no longer exists.

Creatures with backbones, called **vertebrates**, were another important development during this time. All those new body parts allowed these new organisms to swim, hunt, burrow, hide, and defend themselves.

> **During this time, all life on Earth was still in the ocean.**

But then, approximately 470 million years ago, plant life gradually moved out of the water. Now remember, plants didn't suddenly uproot themselves one day and replant themselves on land. Instead, they crept out of the water slowly, slowly, slowly during a very long period of time.

Once plants established themselves on land, they diversified, and many new plant species appeared. This was important to **evolution** because the presence of plants on land allowed for the emergence of land animals. The first were insects. Then, **reptiles** and **amphibians** appeared. By the end of the Paleozoic era, life could be found on land and in the sea.

THE MESOZOIC ERA

At the end of the Paleozoic era, a **mass extinction** was caused by massive volcanic eruptions during the course of millions of years. More than 95 percent of life on Earth was wiped out! However, some species did survive, new species evolved, and biodiversity increased once again.

A Postosuchus skeleton from the Triassic period during the Mesozoic Era
credit: Dallas Krentzel (CC BY 2.0)

During the Mesozoic era, flying reptiles appeared. Amphibians—including snakes, frogs, and crocodiles—thrived. The Mesozoic era was also the time of the dinosaurs. These powerful creatures dominated the land. In the sea, giant reptiles ruled. During this era, the first mammals also emerged, as well as birds and flowering plants.

Today, no dinosaurs roam the hills and streets. That's because at the end of the Mesozoic era, another mass extinction took place. That time, about 66 million years ago, an asteroid approximately 6 miles wide slammed into Earth. It hit with such force it caused earthquakes, **tsunamis**, and a shock wave of heat.

DID YOU KNOW?

Of all the species on Earth today, close to two-thirds are bacteria!

The impact of the asteroid released gases and sent massive amounts of **ejecta** into the air. As the ejecta rained back down to Earth, it caused wildfires. The smoke from these fires, combined with the debris in the atmosphere, blocked out the sun. All of this caused extreme changes in **climate** and the **extinction** of approximately 50 percent of all life on Earth.

WORDS TO KNOW

megafauna: very large animals.

primate: any member of a group of animals that includes humans, apes, and monkeys.

ape: a large, tailless primate such as a gorilla, chimpanzee, or orangutan.

ancestor: someone from your family who lived before you.

microbe: a tiny living or nonliving thing.

microbiome: a community of microbes.

CENOZOIC ERA

After the asteroid strike, life recovered once again. Without the dinosaurs around, other animals thrived. Species of mammals became more diverse, and soon they were the ones dominating the landscape.

Can you imagine a 7-foot-tall kangaroo hopping around? Or a huge armadillo-like creature the size of a small car ambling about? This was called a glyptodon! There were also giant ground sloths, mastodons, and saber-toothed cats. These huge creatures are called **megafauna**.

Another major event during the Cenozoic era was the evolution of the first **primates**, roughly 60 million years ago. That led to the evolution of **apes** and humans.

Human Evolution

It is true that humans are primates, but the last common **ancestor** we shared with bonobos and chimpanzees lived between 5 and 7 million years ago. This evolution of humans from primates happened very, very slowly— during the course of millions of years. A chimpanzee didn't simply give birth to a human baby! We can never know for sure how humans diverged from chimps, but gradually, small changes took place. These changes included the ability to stand and walk upright. Being able to stand allowed these primitive humans to spot danger in the grasslands of Africa where they lived. Early humans became larger and stronger and had bigger brains than their early ancestors. This led to their ability to use tools and fire. They also learned how to communicate and plan.

Soil

If you pick up a teaspoon of soil, you will have in your hand up to 10 billion live organisms! And among those organisms in that gram of soil you might find between 50,000 and 83,000 different species of bacteria and fungi! That's right—every gram of soil has an entire world of microorganisms. Plus, if you took a different handful of soil from a spot a few feet away, the collection of **microbes** could be quite different. The same is true if you dig down a few feet into the ground.

Scientists call this community of microbes a soil **microbiome**. Within these microbiomes, research has found that the organisms are interconnected and that each benefits the others. And, the healthier the community of microbes, the healthier the soil is. And the healthier the soil is, the healthier the ecosystem is. Scientists are still learning about interactions between the microbes and how they function in the soil.

What they do know is that fostering healthy soil can help agricultural production without the use of manmade chemicals and fertilizers, which can be harmful to the environment. Not only does this approach to farming help promote biodiversity in the soil, it also helps to prevent biodiversity loss due to chemical poisoning.

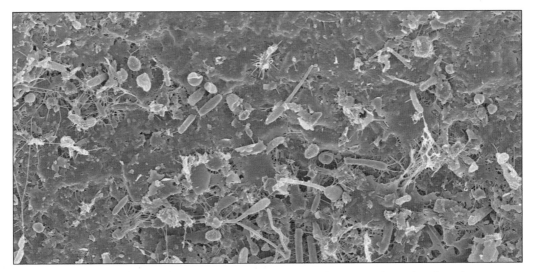

A natural community of bacteria growing in soil, on a single grain of sand

credit: Image courtesy of the Lewis Lab at Northeastern University
Image created by Anthony D'Onofrio, William H. Fowle, Eric J. Stewart and Kim Lewis (CC BY 2.0)

WORDS TO KNOW

DNA: the substance found in the cells of every living thing that determines everything about us, including whether we are human, an insect, or something else; have blue eyes or brown; are right- or left-handed; and every other trait that makes us who we are.

variations: the behavioral and physical differences among members of a species.

Scientists have discovered that the very first primitive human species made tools more than 3 million years ago.

Between 1.8 million and 800,000 years ago, they began to use fire for cooking and heating. After that, humans evolved more quickly—their brains became more complex and they developed language. Our species, *Homo sapiens*, evolved in Africa 200,000 years ago. And here we are today!

DID YOU KNOW?

We humans share almost 99 percent of our **DNA** with chimpanzees and bonobos.

HOW DID THIS HAPPEN?

You might be wondering how life on Earth went from a small, single-celled organism to the amazing biodiversity we have today. The answer is evolution.

Evolution is the process by which organisms have diversified and changed through time. The evolution of a new species is a complex process that usually happens during an extremely long period of time. It occurs when two populations of a species develop differently. They may have started out the same, but as time passes, the two populations become more and more different.

Check out this interactive video that tells the story of human origins. The interactive timeline traces humans' roots back 7 million years.

🔎 Becoming Human

Eventually, the differences are so great that a member of one population cannot produce offspring with a member of the other population. When that happens, scientists consider the two populations to be two separate species.

Members of the same species evolve differently due to a number of factors. One of the most critical has to do with the **variations** within a species.

 Explore the deep history of life on Earth in this interactive timeline from Biointeractive. Click the different pictures for more information. Some of the pop-ups also have videos. What do you notice about the evolution of life on Earth?

🔎 Biointeractive Deep History

Look around you. People are different, even if they are related to one another. You might have dark hair, while your sibling has light hair. That same sibling might have green eyes while yours are brown. Maybe one cousin is a terrific artist and another cousin excels at sports. Other variations are ones we can't see, such as blood type or being a carrier of certain genetic diseases.

Zebras evolved into striped creatures that can't be seen very well in the grasslands where they live!

WORDS TO KNOW

camouflage: the colors or patterns that allow a plant or animal to blend in with its environment.

predator: an animal or plant that kills and eats another animal.

adaptation: the changes a plant or animal has made to help it survive.

natural selection: one of the basic means of evolution in which organisms that are well-adapted to their environment are better able to survive, reproduce, and pass along their useful traits to offspring.

eukaryote: a class of organisms composed of one or more cells that contains a nucleus.

archaea: single-celled microbes that live in extremely harsh environments.

In nature, these variations are important to survival. For example, if one animal has a fur color that makes it better able to **camouflage** itself and avoid **predators** than others of its species, it will live longer. And it will produce more offspring and pass along those useful traits to those offspring. Individuals without the useful variations aren't as likely to survive or reproduce.

The first person to bring attention to evolution was a man named Charles Darwin. His extensive observations of variations and **adaptations** in nature led him to develop the theory of evolution by **natural selection** in the mid-1800s. His theory explains how species change through time and how all species have evolved from simple life forms.

Bizarre Biodiversity

Leafy Sea Dragon: Found in the waters east and south of Australia, these fish have leaf-like appendages that help them camouflage themselves in kelp and seaweed.

credit: Jim G from Silicon Valley, CA, USA (CC BY 2.0)

Scientists have created a detailed Tree of Life that shows the relationships between all species on the planet. The tree has a main trunk, branching off into three smaller trunks. These branches are named **Eukaryotes** (that's our branch!), Bacteria, and **Archaea**. Each branch on the tree represents a different species.

This interactive Tree of Life that will allow you to explore the relationship between the almost 2 million known species of life on Earth.

PS

🔍 OneZoom

Since that first tree was published, scientists have continued to study biodiversity on Earth and add information to the Tree of Life. Advances in science have also helped these scientists to add detail.

DID YOU KNOW?

According to scientists, we have yet to discover more than 90 percent of species, and many may go extinct before we even know about them!

The tree is very complex, but if you take a close look, you can see how you are related to all other life on Earth!

Or you can find out how hippopotamuses are related to whales. And how elephants are related to hyrax—a furry, small, rodent-like animal.

Even just one look at the Tree of Life reveals the vast amount biodiversity on Earth and the fact that we are all related. From those very first single-celled organisms, life has evolved and now inhabits all parts of the earth.

ESSENTIAL QUESTION

How has life on Earth become so diverse?

CREATE A TREE OF LIFE

The Tree of Life is an excellent way to help us understand how all life on Earth is related. Imagine that you are assigned the task of creating a tree of life for young, elementary-aged kids to introduce them to the topic.

▶ Investigate the Tree of Life and its three main branches. Then, design and create a simplified tree of life. You may want to create a **collage** or draw a picture. You could also try to make a three-dimensional model. No matter how you do it, the goal is to represent the relationships among species so that young children can understand them. Try to include a variety of species.

▶ Evaluate your tree. Will young children be able to see and understand your simplified tree of life? How did you decide what to add to your tree and what to leave out? What else could you add to it? Which branch was the most difficult to create?

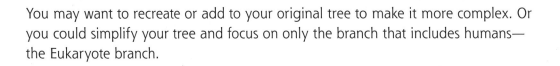

Phylogenetic Tree of Life

Bacteria   Archaea   Eucarya

Green Filamentous bacteria
Spirochetes
Gram positives
Proteobacteria
Cyanobacteria
Planctomyces
Bacteroides Cytophaga
Thermotoga
Aquifex

Methanosarcina
Methanobacterium
Methanococcus
T. celer
Thermoproteus
Pyrodicticum

Entamoebae
Halophiles

Myxomycota
Animalia
Fungi
Plantae
Ciliates
Flagellates
Trichomonads
Microsporidia
Diplomonads

Try This!

You may want to recreate or add to your original tree to make it more complex. Or you could simplify your tree and focus on only the branch that includes humans—the Eukaryote branch.

WORDS TO KNOW

collage: a work of art made up of different pieces of material.

CREATE A TABLETOP BIOSPHERE

Ideas for supplies: airtight jar (at least 24-ounce size), pebbles or sand, soil, plants with roots still attached, distilled water, insect

A biosphere is a perfect environment where life can exist. Earth itself is a biosphere, with all parts in perfect balance with one another. You can design and build your own mini-biosphere, a closed ecosystem. Before you begin, predict what you think the challenges will be in creating a perfectly balanced environment where all life can thrive.

❯ **Make sure that the jar is completely clean.** Begin with a layer of pebbles or sand on the bottom.

❯ **Add about 2 inches of soil.** Plant two or three small plants in the soil. Add enough water to the biosphere so that the soil is damp but not saturated. Include an insect or two. Seal the biosphere with the lid and place it near a light source or window.

❯ **You may want to take a photo of your biosphere or draw a sketch.** Start a scientific method worksheet, then observe your biosphere every day. Take notes on what you see and what has changed. Were you able to create a successful biosphere? If so, what factors led to the success of the biosphere? If not, what was out of balance?

Try This!

You can create a tabletop biosphere in many, many other ways. If you were successful the first time, consider a more complex biosphere. Or perhaps an aquatic biosphere. Do some research on the internet for this. One great set of instructions is on the Make e-magazine site.

🔎 make biosphere

EXPLORE ADAPTATIONS

Adaptations allow organisms to thrive in their environment. Organisms must be able to find food and shelter and avoid predators. Some of these adaptations are physical and others are behavioral.

❯ Take your science journal outside and select a species. You might choose a tree, insect, bird, turtle, or something else. Spend some time observing the species. Identify key adaptations of the organism.

❯ Create a chart of the physical and behavioral adaptations you see. Then, consider how each of these helps the species to survive.

Name of Species: _____   **Location:** _____

Physical Adaptation	How it helps
Behavioral Adaptation	How it helps

Consider This

Think about how well adapted the species you observed is. What do you predict would happen to the species if something in the environment changed? Also consider what you might observe about the species in a different season. What do you believe the threats to this species might be? Finally, study other species near you. If you chose a bird for the first observation, perhaps look at a plant or insect. Compare and contrast the adaptations of the species.

WORDS TO KNOW

physical: relating to the body.

behavioral: having to do with the way an organism acts and interacts with its environment and other organisms in order to survive.

SOIL SAMPLE

Soil is a wondrous universe all of its own. Using a microscope and soil samples, you can experience this amazing world of biodiversity just below our feet.

▶ **Start by gathering several clean containers and clean spoons.** That ensures that you do not contaminate the samples you take. Select a spot in the park, by a pond, or at school to collect a soil sample. Or you might want to take one sample from each of these places!

▶ **Use a different container and spoon each time you collect a sample.** Make sure to label each container with the location where the soil was taken.

▶ **Once you have your sample or samples, observe them under a microscope.** If you do not have a high-powered microscope at home, check at your school or local library. Be sure to use a different, clean microscope slide for each sample. Record your observations either with sketches or descriptions.

Worms

Soil needs a variety of microorganisms to stay healthy. It also needs worms. They may be small, but they are mighty. That's why gardeners and farmers love them so much. Worms are like tiny farm hands, working to increase the amount of oxygen and water that get into the soil. The burrows that worms make create a natural, underground drainage system. Those same burrows allow air to flow into the ground.

Consider This

How many different types of microorganisms did you observe? Were you surprised by this? If you took numerous samples, how did the biodiversity vary between the samples? How was it the same? You may also want to consider taking samples at different times of year, from different depths in the same spot, or from places farther away from your home.

Chapter 2

BIODIVERSITY
EVERYWHERE

Everywhere you look, everywhere on Earth, you will find life. Biodiversity exists in every corner of the planet. Some examples of biodiversity you can see. A lot you cannot. Biodiversity is found in large biomes as well as microbiomes.

Life thrives in places you might expect, such as in rainforests or oceans. But it also thrives in unlikely places, including deserts and the Arctic. Biodiversity is even found in ice and volcanoes. Life is everywhere!

While biodiversity is found in every corner of the planet, it is not evenly distributed, or spread around. Colder ecosystems tend to have less species diversity than warmer ones. The study of the distribution of species, and the patterns of distribution across the planet, is called **biogeography**.

ESSENTIAL QUESTION

Where is biodiversity found?

DISTRIBUTION

In biogeography, scientists look at species diversity in an area. They also look at the size of the population of each species, along with other factors. This helps scientists to better understand the factors that have shaped biodiversity in Earth's history and to predict how biodiversity will respond to our changing planet.

Biodiversity is unevenly distributed because species rely on many different factors to survive. Abiotic factors such as temperature, **precipitation**, and **geography** all affect species diversity and species populations in different areas. Some species live in fresh water, while others live in salt water. Some species thrive in extremely cold climates, while others are adapted to living in hot climates. Still others live in very wet, humid climates, while others are adapted to dry climates.

The darker red places on the map have the highest human population density.
credit: daysleeperrr (CC0 1.0)

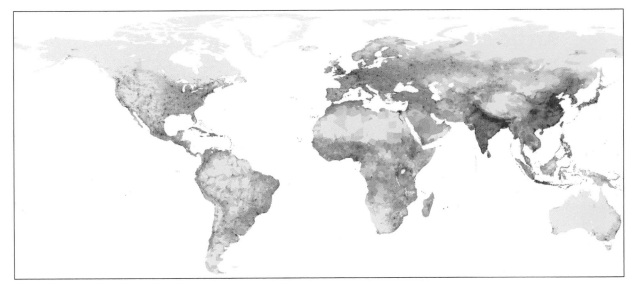

WORDS TO KNOW

polar regions: the areas of the earth around the North and South Poles, within the Arctic and Antarctic Circles.

temperate zone: the area of the earth that lies between the tropics and the polar regions.

tropical zone: the area of the earth around the equator.

tundra: a treeless Arctic region that is permanently frozen below the top layer of soil.

lichen: a plant-like organism made of algae and fungus that grows on solid surfaces such as rocks or trees.

savanna: a dry, rolling grassland with scattered shrubs and trees.

Biotic factors also affect species diversity and species populations. In places with high biodiversity, more life can be supported than in places with low biodiversity. Life depends on other life to survive.

Even the distribution pattern of humans is uneven, affected by both abiotic and biotic factors. Few people live in the cold **polar regions**. The closer to the warmer **temperate zone** and even warmer **tropical zone** you look, however, the more people there are.

There are also few people who live in extreme desert climates or high mountain ecosystems. More people live in areas with ample rainfall and moderate temperatures suitable for farming. Humans tend to live in areas that have many resources, which include biodiversity. These biotic factors are important to people for food, shelter, fuel, and clothing.

DID YOU KNOW?

Rainforests cover less than 2 percent of the earth's surface but host more than 50 percent of Earth's biodiversity!

Arctic Adaptations

All organisms living in polar regions have adaptations that allow them to survive in the harsh climate. The polar bear has a thick fur coat and a layer of blubber to keep it warm. Snowshoe hares have fur coats as well, but they also cluster together for warmth. Plants in the polar region stay close together, too! They are low-lying plants and can photosynthesize under a layer of snow. Flowering plants have a brief seasonal cycle, so they can produce flowers quickly once warmer weather arrives. These plants are also drought-tolerant. Even the microorganisms must be adapted to withstand the cold in the polar regions. Some cyanobacteria, researchers have discovered, wrap themselves in a complex coating made of sugar that protects their cells from freezing.

ON LAND

If you visit the Arctic **tundra**, you would find low species diversity. You might see a large herd of caribou, a polar bear, or an Arctic fox in the Arctic region. In the Antarctic, you will find several species of penguins and seals. You will also see moss, **lichen**, and other small plants in these polar regions during their summer season.

Countless microorganisms also survive in the polar regions. Every species in these regions, from the largest polar bear to those tiny microbes, is well-adapted to the harsh environment and is an important part of those ecosystems.

As you move south from the Arctic, species diversity increases. You will see a greater variety of plants, animals, fungi, bacteria, and other microorganisms as you pass through forests, **savannas**, and grasslands in the temperate zone. As you get closer to the equator in the tropics, the biodiversity is even greater.

The blue poison dart frog lives in the rainforest.
credit: Michael Gäbler (CC BY 3.0)

Rainforests have the greatest biodiversity on Earth. The warm, tropical regions support millions of different species. If you stood in the middle of a rainforest, you might see howler monkeys, toucans, sloths, tree frogs, bromeliad plants, orchids, leafcutter ants, sharpshooter leafhoppers, and countless other species. In the Amazon rainforest alone, scientists have identified more than 40,000 plant species, 400 mammals, 1,300 birds, close to 400 reptiles, more than 400 amphibians, and approximately 3,000 species of fish. That doesn't even include the microorganisms!

WORDS TO KNOW

endemic: a plant or animal that is native to only a certain area.

producer: a part of a food chain that includes all plants that make their own food through photosynthesis.

food chain: a community of plants and animals where each is eaten by another higher up in the chain.

nutrients: substances in food and soil that living things need to live and grow.

salinity: the amount of salt in water.

Endemic Species

Some species are found in only one place on the planet—they are called **endemic** species. These species are usually limited to a certain ecosystem, small or large, because they are uniquely adapted to that environment. Because of this specialization, these species cannot move to other habitats. The wet-rock physa, a snail the size of a pinhead, is one endemic species living only in Zion National Park in Utah. The Texas blind salamander is found exclusively in water-filled caves in one part of Texas. And the flowering Holgrem's buckwheat plant can be seen only in Great Basin National Park in Nevada.

One explanation for greater species diversity in the tropics is the abundance of both sunlight and rain, as well as warm temperatures. In that region, the sun is overhead for the same number of hours a day all year round. Therefore, the sun's energy supports the continual growth of **producers** of the **food chain**—plants—all year round. Regular rainfall and moderate temperatures also help the producers to grow. This plant life then supports other life in the region.

Longer periods of tropical conditions over greater areas of the planet throughout Earth's history are another reason biodiversity is unevenly distributed. Species have lived in tropical climates longer than in cooler ones. These tropical species have had longer to adapt and evolve into new species.

Bizarre Biodiversity

Archer Fish: The archer fish got its name because it takes aim at an insect above the water surface and shoots a mouthful of water at it to knock the insect into the water to eat it.

credit: James St. John (CC BY 2.0)

AQUATIC LIFE

Welcome to a rainforest of the sea—a coral reef!

Life on Earth is not found just on land. Lakes, streams, wetlands, ponds, and oceans are full of biodiversity, too. In the ocean alone, during the Census for Marine Life in the early 2000s, scientists documented 250,000 known marine species, and that count doesn't include microbes. Scientists estimate that another 750,000 species, plus more than a billion species of microbes, live in the ocean.

Just as on land, many different ecosystems exist within the ocean. And just as on land, life in the ocean is not evenly distributed among them. This distribution is affected by many factors, including temperature, sunlight, **nutrients**, **salinity**, and water pressure.

DID YOU KNOW?

Biodiversity is so great on some tropical reefs that there may be 1,000 different species within 1 square meter.

Some places in the ocean, such as coral reefs in the tropics, are full of life. In fact, because of their biodiversity, coral reefs are often called the rainforests of the sea.

33

WORDS TO KNOW

estuary: a body of water where a river meets the ocean, with a mix of fresh water and salt water.

chemosynthesis: the process some organisms use to create energy from chemicals instead of the sun.

extremophile: an organism that thrives in environments that most other life forms cannot live in.

permafrost: permanently frozen subsoil and rock just beneath the surface of the ground.

global warming: an increase in the average temperature of the earth's atmosphere, enough to cause climate change.

dormant: in a state of rest or inactivity.

infectious: illness that is spread by germs or viruses.

Check out this interactive site and find information about the biodiversity found in the earth's oceans, as well as links to explore further.

ρ marine shining sea

Estuaries are places where rivers meet the ocean. They are very productive ecosystems, providing food, nurseries, and migration stopovers for many marine species. In estuaries, you might find mangrove trees or marshes, sea otters and herons, or many other species such as fish, seahorses, crabs, and oysters.

Other places in the ocean, such as colder waters, places far from land, and the very deep parts of the ocean, have very low biodiversity. Yet, as you will learn, even though the biodiversity is low, there is still life in these extreme places.

Census of Marine Life

During a 10-year period, scientists from 80 different countries collaborated to record biodiversity in the oceans. They also looked at the distribution and populations of species. To collect this information, more than 2,700 scientists participated in 540 different marine expeditions. They explored coral reefs, shorelines, the deep-sea floor, open ocean, underwater mountains called seamounts, the Arctic and Antarctic regions, and more. Their work contributes to our understanding of oceans past and present, which can help with future planning to protect marine species. Despite the scope of the project, however, 95 percent of the ocean is still unexplored. Because of that, scientists estimate that 91 percent of all ocean biodiversity has not yet been formally identified and recorded!

Not All Life Needs Oxygen or Sunlight

Humans would certainly consider an environment without oxygen or sunlight extreme. So would most of the other species on Earth. However, not all life needs oxygen or sunlight to thrive. Some microorganisms living at the bottom of the deep ocean, for example, use a process called **chemosynthesis** to convert chemicals into energy instead of using sunlight for photosynthesis. These microbes are found living near hydrothermal vents that spew the chemicals the microorganisms use. Other microorganisms, such as some species of bacteria, are anaerobic. They survive in environments with little or no oxygen, soil, and water, and even inside living animals! Scientists also discovered microscopic multi-cellular animals called Loricifera living in the oxygen-free sediment at the bottom of the Mediterranean Sea.

EXTREMOPHILES

Of all the places on Earth you may not expect to find life, ice, volcanoes, and the deep, deep ocean might come to mind. But even in these extreme environments, scientists have discovered life—hardy organisms called **extremophiles** thrive in environments where most other species could not exist.

Some of these extremophiles are found in or under ice in the polar regions. In both the Arctic and Antarctic ice, researchers have found living bacteria. The populations are small, but they are there and alive despite the low-nutrient, low-temperature environment.

Some bacteria and viruses have been locked away in the ice for tens of thousands of years! As glaciers retreat and **permafrost** melts due to **global warming**, ancient bacteria and viruses that were **dormant** are making a comeback. Scientists are concerned that some of these life forms that have survived in this extreme environment for hundreds of thousands of years could become a source of deadly **infectious** diseases today.

WORDS TO KNOW

antifreeze: a liquid that is added to a second liquid to lower the temperature at which the second liquid freezes.

terrestrial: related to land.

toxic: poisonous.

Lakes buried beneath the ice are another place that extremophiles live in the polar regions. Locked under more than 2 miles of ice in eastern Antarctica is Lake Vostok. The water in this lake—roughly the size of Lake Ontario on the U.S. and Canadian border—has been trapped underneath the ice for more than 15 million years. No light reaches the water. Yet scientists discovered a unique ecosystem in the water, based on minerals in the lake and rock instead of on sunlight. The biodiversity in this lake includes fungi, Archaea, thousands of bacteria, and other microbes.

DID YOU KNOW?

In 2005, scientists at NASA were able to revive bacteria that had been trapped for 32,000 years in a frozen pond in Alaska.

The vivid colors around the Grand Pragmatic Spring at Yellowstone Park are caused by the microbes that live there!

credit: Jim Peaco, National Park Service

Bizarre Biodiversity

Icefish: These Antarctic fish have blood that acts like **antifreeze**. They can withstand cold temperatures that would freeze other fish.

credit: Valerie Loeb, NOAA

On the other end of the temperature spectrum, very hot places have biodiversity, too. One such place is in Yellowstone National Park. The hot springs and mud pots there are home to a variety of microbes. The temperatures in the hot springs and mud pots are too hot for humans to touch. But the organisms living there survive in temperatures hotter than 175 degrees Fahrenheit (79 degrees Celsius). That's almost boiling!

Researchers have also explored in and around volcanoes, which are hot and acidic with few nutrients. Despite the harsh environment, they have discovered bacteria, fungi, and other organisms living around volcanoes.

However, the inside of an active, **terrestrial** volcano is another story. The lava is simply too hot to support life. Remember how the earth didn't have life at first because the entire planet was covered in molten rock? It had to cool for millions of years before the first life forms appeared.

Many volcanoes are found on the sea floor as well. Near the deep-sea

Caves are another extreme environment that contain fragile ecosystems and sustain rich biodiversity.

(PS) **Go on a cave exploration by watching this National Geographic video.**

🔎 Nat Geo inside caves

volcanoes and hydrothermal vents, the water spewing out can be as hot as 660 degrees Fahrenheit (316 degrees Celsius). It is also full of **toxic** chemicals. Yet scientists have discovered bacteria, shrimp, worms, crabs, barnacles, and more thriving in this extreme environment. In some ways, these volcanoes and vents are oases for life in the ocean.

BIODIVERSITY

The deep, deep ocean is another extreme environment on Earth where life can be found. The Mariana Trench is the deepest part of the ocean in the world—it is 7 miles below the surface of the ocean. No light or oxygen exists down there, it is very cold, and the water pressure is tremendous. However, researchers have discovered bizarre creatures thriving there, including the **bioluminescent** anglerfish, crabs, and hundreds of types of microorganisms. Even the mud on the sea floor contains more than 200 different microorganisms.

DID YOU KNOW?

More than 17,000 species live in the deep ocean, where there is no light.

As you will learn, all this biodiversity found everywhere on the planet has a part in keeping Earth's ecosystems healthy. Biodiversity matters!

A striped anglerfish

credit: SEFSC Pascagoula Laboratory; Collection of Brandi Noble, NOAA/NMFS/SEFSC

Beaches are a bit of an extreme environment. There isn't much space. Sometimes there's water, other times the tide goes out and there's none. And waves are constantly pounding on the ecosystem. But, as in any ecosystem, the species that live there are well adapted to the environment. Microscopic organisms are small enough to move around between the grains of sand. They have other adaptations to protect them from pounding waves and to keep them from washing away.

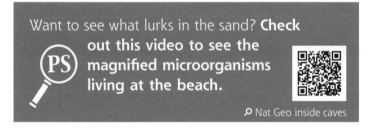

Want to see what lurks in the sand? **Check out this video to see the magnified microorganisms living at the beach.**

PS

🔎 Nat Geo inside caves

Sand is also home to billions of bacteria. A 2017 study revealed that on one grain of sand there may be between 10,000 and 100,000 microorganisms. To get a better idea of what that means, a grain of sand has more microorganisms than Helena, Montana, has residents!

Now that we've explored some of the places where biodiversity can be found, let's turn our attention to why this is important. In the next chapter, we'll find out why biodiversity matters so much to all life on Earth!

ESSENTIAL QUESTION

Where is biodiversity found?

MAKE BIOGAS

Every organism in an ecosystem plays an important role. Even when an organism dies, it helps the ecosystem function because it provides food for other organisms. Some of the organisms to benefit are microorganisms, which occasionally feed on dead or decaying matter. We can't see these tiny organisms, but you can see the results of their work.

▶ Fill a plastic bottle with organic matter, such as dead leaves and compost.

▶ Stretch an uninflated balloon over the opening of the bottle. Make sure there is a tight seal between the bottle and the balloon. Place the bottle near heat or in the sun.

▶ What do you think will happen? Why? Start a scientific method worksheet in you science journal. Include your predictions. During the next week or so, observe the bottle and balloon. Record your observations in your journal.

Consider This

Reproduce the experiment using different organic materials and different light and temperature conditions. What happens? How are the results different from your original experiment?

Why do you think you got the results you did? What was going on in the bottle? What were the microorganisms doing? Do some research to see how scientists apply this knowledge to solve real-world problems.

VISIT A WETLAND

Wetlands are found all over the world. Once thought of as wastelands to be drained, dredged, and filled, wetlands are now recognized for the important **ecosystem services** they provide, including purifying water and protecting against flooding and erosion. There are many kinds of wetlands—swamps, lagoons, bogs, tidal marshes, and more. They can be enormous, such as the Prairie Pothole Region in the northern Great Plains, or as tiny as a puddle. No matter their size or location, these wetlands are home to great biodiversity.

> **Do some research to find a wetland near you.** Take along your science journal, binoculars, a camera, and a friend.

> **How many different species do you see?** List them in your journal. Look for plants, birds, mammals, fish, reptiles, amphibians, and insects.

> **Find a comfortable place to sit quietly for 10 to 15 minutes.** Observe what happens when you are quiet. Add the additional species you spot to your list. Take pictures or draw sketches of the biodiversity you find in the wetland. Also note the abiotic factors that influence the ecosystem.

Consider This

What species do you think might be in the wetland that you cannot see? Consider taking a water sample home to look at more closely under a microscope. (NOTE: Ask an adult for permission and use caution around water.) Using your notes, consider how all the biotic and abiotic factors in this habitat are interconnected. This may require more research or another visit the area to talk to a park ranger, scientist, or other expert. Determine the ecosystem services provided by the wetland you visited and predict what might happen if that wetland was damaged or destroyed.

WORDS TO KNOW

wetlands: low areas filled with water, such as a marsh or swamp.

ecosystem services: the important benefits provided by ecosystems to keep the earth's air, water, and soil healthy.

THE HUMAN MICROBIOME

Even the human body is home to millions of microbes. The community of microbes varies depending on where they live in your body, just as species vary within different ecosystems on the planet. Microbial communities also vary from person to person. While this may sound a bit disgusting at first, these microbes are very important to your health. Just as they do in other ecosystems, microbes help keep your body in balance. You are healthier with them than without them!

> **One of the most important and complex microbiomes in the human body is in the gut.** Research the human microbiome in your own gut. Find out what factors influence the different types of microbes there. Some factors are out of our control, such as genetics, but other factors we can control. Learn what you can do to promote a healthy gut microbiome and to keep it balanced.

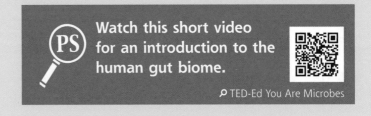

PS Watch this short video for an introduction to the human gut biome.

🔎 TED-Ed You Are Microbes

> **Make a chart of the things you do that are good for your gut microbiome and things that need work.** Based on your findings, make a plan to promote a healthier gut. Consider, for example, focusing on what you eat, how much water you drink, and the time you spend outdoors. Think about getting friends or family members to join you.

> **Before you change your routine or your diet, take notes about how you feel most of the time, morning, midday, and in the evening.** Also make note of how you feel after a meal. Full? Energized? Sluggish? Do you have a stomachache? Cramps? Follow your plan of action faithfully for a full week.

Sand

When you look at a sandy beach, it may seem like it has little biodiversity. You may come across a crab or shore birds, but not much else. But if you magnify a handful of sand, you will discover millions of organisms. Just as in soil, these microorganisms in the sand live in their own unique ecosystem. And the organisms you find will vary between beaches and will also vary depending on their location on a single beach.

Magnified Microbiome!

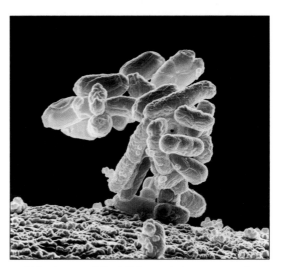

This cluster of E. Coli bacteria is an example of a microbe that thrives in beach sand.

credit: U.S. Department of Agriculture

Consider This

How do you feel since you've focused on promoting healthy gut microbes? Better? Worse? Explain. Was making changes in your routine easy or difficult? Can you keep it up? Sometimes it takes a few weeks to develop new habits. Keep following your plan of action for a full month. How do you feel after that much time? Is it hard not to cheat?

How much do you know about your own microbiome? This online quiz will test your knowledge and present valuable facts about the microbes in your body.

🔎 American Museum human biome quiz

SAMPLE THE WATER

Water is alive with microbes! The types of microbes you find in water will, of course, vary depending on where you take the water sample from.

Caution: Be careful around water—always have an adult with you!

❯ **Collect water from five different places near you.** Each time you collect a sample, carefully label each with the location the sample was taken from, the time of day, and the date.

❯ **At home, predict what you will see when you observe the samples closely.** Start a scientific method worksheet in your science journal.

❯ **First, look at the sample with just your eyes.** Can you see anything in the water? Now, look at each sample separately under the microscope. What microorganisms are in the water sample? Make a chart to record your findings, including a quick sketch. Note the behavior of the different organisms.

Consider This

How are the five samples the same? Different? Is this surprising? Why or why not? You could repeat the experiment, taking samples from the same places but at different times of the year. Compare the differences. Alternatively, you could take different samples from the same water source in different areas of that source. For example, in a pond, take samples from different places near the shore, from deeper in the water, or even, if possible, from the center of the pond. Ask an adult before heading out to deeper water, and always wear a life vest.

DID YOU KNOW?

Of all the water on Earth, less than 1 percent is accessible freshwater and suitable for filtering to use as drinking water.

Chapter 3

WHY BIODIVERSITY
MATTERS

It can be difficult to see how nature and biodiversity are important. It is especially hard because in today's modern world, we live in human-created environments, surrounded mostly by other humans. Everything is controlled, from where our food comes from and the temperature of the indoor air to the water that comes out of the tap.

ESSENTIAL QUESTION

Why is biodiversity so important?

Many of us don't interact regularly with nature because we spend so much time in that controlled environment. Yet behind the scenes, biodiversity keeps our entire planet healthy and balanced. Let's find out how it happens.

WORDS TO KNOW

pollinate: to transfer pollen from the male parts of flowers to the female parts so that flowers can make seeds. Pollen is a powder made by flowers that is needed for the flower to make a seed.

decompose: to rot or decay.

organic matter: decaying plants and animals.

spore: a structure produced by fungi that sprouts and grows into a new fungus.

food web: a network of connected food chains.

consumer: an organism that eats other organisms.

decomposer: an organism that breaks down organic matter.

algae: a simple organism found in water that is like a plant but without roots, stems, or leaves.

herbivore: an animal that eats only plants.

carnivore: an animal that eats only other animals.

ECOSYSTEM STABILITY

To start, biodiversity is important to ecosystems, because within an ecosystem, every species has a role to play. Species sometimes compete with other species for resources. They may eat other species or be eaten by them. Some species provide shelter. Many different species help scatter seeds or **pollinate** plants. Other species help clean water or improve the soil. Some control pests. Others **decompose organic matter**. Yet others help to physically alter the ecosystem in ways that keep it healthy for all species.

The relationships are complex, but each species in an ecosystem plays its role, keeping the system in balance.

Bizarre Biodiversity

Starfish Stinkhorn are fungi that produce a stinky slime to attract insects that help the fungi disperse **spores** for reproduction.

This rabbit is an herbivore, one type of consumer.

One way to think of the interconnectedness of living things is to look at food chains and **food webs**. A food chain is a series of species that rely on the one before for survival. Food chains combine in food webs.

In any ecosystem, you will find producers, **consumers**, and **decomposers**. The first link in the chain is the producer. Producers are plants, which get their energy from the sun to make their own food through photosynthesis. Trees, flowers, shrubs, kelp, grasses, **algae**, and cyanobacteria are all examples of producers.

These producers are eaten by **herbivores**, one type of consumer. Another type of consumer is the **carnivore**.

DID YOU KNOW?

Carnivorous plants such as the Venus flytrap eat insects! Whenever anything touches the hairs on the inside of the plant, the two lobes snap shut, trapping the unlucky insect inside.

carbon: an element that is found in all life on Earth and in coal, petroleum, and diamonds.

keystone species: a species that plays an essential role in an ecosystem, and without which the ecosystem would be greatly altered.

ecosystem engineers: species that greatly alter an ecosystem by creating, modifying, maintaining, or destroying it.

refuge: a place that provides protection or safety.

Decomposers live off dead plants and animals. They help break down the plants and animals into gases such as **carbon** and nitrogen. These gases are then released back into the air, water, or soil. Decomposers are the ultimate recyclers!

A simple food chain might begin with a producer such as grass. The grass is eaten by an herbivore, perhaps a rabbit. The rabbit, in turn, is eaten by a carnivore—let's say, a hawk. Eventually, the hawk will die and be broken down by bacteria. Energy and nutrients are passed from one organism to the next in this ecosystem.

However, these food chains do not exist on their own. Instead, they are part of a food web of interconnected food chains.

The example of the grass, rabbit, hawk, and bacteria is just one path energy and nutrients can take in that ecosystem. The grass might also be eaten by herbivores other than the rabbit. The rabbit could also eat other plants besides the grass. And the rabbit might be eaten by a different carnivore, such as a fox. The hawk could eat other animals in addition to the rabbit.

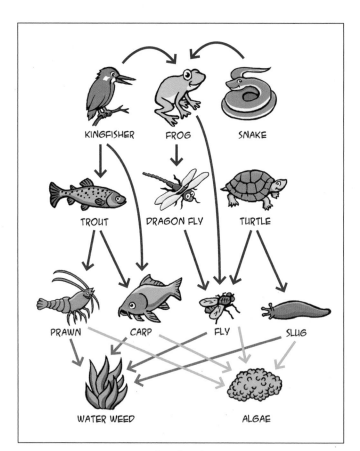

Food web

Alligators: Keepers of the Everglades

American alligators are often misunderstood as fearsome, prehistoric creatures. They are so much more! In the Everglades ecosystem in Florida, the alligators are a **keystone species**. They are also **ecosystem engineers**. Prior to the dry season, when most of the water disappears, the alligators dig holes. These holes hold water throughout the dry season and provide **refuge** for many other species. Without those alligator holes, these other species would not survive.

In this way, the different pathways, or food chains, are all connected to each other, forming a web. It shows us how all species in an ecosystem are interdependent. Plus, each ecosystem has a different food web. So the more biodiversity an ecosystem has, the more complex the food web is. And the more complex the food web, the more stable the entire ecosystem is. In other words, greater species diversity makes an ecosystem healthier.

But why? Well, if one link in a complex food web disappears, energy has other pathways to follow through the ecosystem. If a species in a complex ecosystem becomes extinct, other species will eat that species' food and the predators of the extinct species will have other species to feed on.

But what happens when an ecosystem is unstable and a species disappears? That's a different story. Take sea otters, for example. Sea otters love to eat sea urchins—they help to keep the urchin population in check. Yet in some areas of the sea, otters have disappeared. What do you think happens to the sea urchin population?

This is a delicious sea urchin!

WORDS TO KNOW

watershed: the land area that drains into a river or a lake.

wastewater: dirty water that has been used by people in their homes, in factories, and in other businesses.

The sea urchin increases because its main predator is gone.

Sea urchins, though, eat kelp. So when the sea urchin population increases, kelp forests begin to disappear. This is a problem for many other species that make their home in the kelp forest. The loss of the kelp forest causes losses of other species. This can lead to the collapse of an entire ecosystem.

Think of it like an orchestra. Imagine you are part of a local orchestra with many talented musicians playing many different instruments. Each musician has a position and plays well. Together, you create beautiful music. Even if one musician is out sick, your orchestra can continue without one instrument. Because of the depth and complexity of your orchestra, it remains stable even with a missing link. There is strength in numbers!

But what happens if two people are out sick? Three? Ten? The music doesn't sound as full and beautiful. If your orchestra loses too many musicians, it will be less stable.

A Natural Water Filter

Nature is so good at filtering water that many towns and cities are now creating artificial wetlands and preserving existing **watersheds** to treat their water. Walnut Cove, North Carolina, was faced with costly repairs for its **wastewater** treatment facility in 1994. Instead, in 1996, the town constructed an artificial wetland to treat wastewater. In 2016, the Walnut Cove facility celebrated 20 years of success. This budget-friendly alternative to traditional facilities is also used by major cities. New York City invested in protecting and conserving the land around the streams, rivers, lakes, and reservoirs in the watersheds that provide most of the city's drinking water. In this case, preserving what was already there worked just as well as creating new wetlands.

The Photo Ark

Photographer Joel Sartore (1962–) was disturbed by biodiversity loss and increased rates of extinction. To capture Earth's biodiversity before it's too late, he decided to build an ark—out of photographs. He began a mission to photograph as many species in captivity as he could before they became extinct. In addition to information on the internet, Sartore has a book published by National Geographic, *The Photo Ark*.

You can look at pictures from the ark at this website.

🔍 Joel Sartore Ark

ECOSYSTEM SERVICES

Not only does biodiversity maintain ecosystem stability, it also performs ecosystem services. These services include providing clean water, clean air, carbon storage, and nutrient recycling. They are the beneficial outcomes of a healthy, functioning ecosystem.

When water moves through a wetland ecosystem, it gets cleaned and filtered. Wetlands are even considered the kidneys of the earth because they are so effective. And just like your own kidneys, wetlands filter waste and pollutants from water before it moves downstream.

WORDS TO KNOW

sediment: material deposited by water, wind, or glaciers.

sedimentation: the process of solid matter settling to the bottom of water.

climate change: a change in long-term weather patterns, which happens through both natural and man-made processes.

phytoplankton: microscopic plants at the base of the marine food web.

Bizarre Biodiversity

Sacoglossan sea slug: Found in the Caribbean Ocean, these sea slugs eat algae, but they also store it to make their own food through photosynthesis!

credit: LASZLO ILYES (CC BY 2.0)

The vegetation in healthy wetlands slows water down, allowing natural **sediment** carried in the water to settle to the bottom. This keeps the sediment from continuing downstream, where it may disrupt other ecosystems or interfere with the natural flow of water. The plants in the wetlands also absorb excess nutrients and pollutants. Some of it is converted to less harmful substances. Some of it is removed through **sedimentation**, as the pollutants remain buried on the bottom of the wetland.

Tiny Ocean Critters Do a Big Job

You've probably heard a lot about the increase in CO_2 in our atmosphere, which has led to global warming and **climate change**. Biodiversity becomes even more important because different organisms draw CO_2 from the air. Yet large plants and trees are not the only ones providing this service. Some of the tiniest species on Earth play a key role. In the ocean, vast numbers of **phytoplankton**, microscopic marine plants, pull CO_2 from the water for photosynthesis just as land plants do. They might be small, but there is strength in numbers! In fact, the phytoplankton in the oceans are responsible for removing as much CO_2 from our atmosphere as land plants do.

Biodiversity helps clean the air, too. Just as plants draw pollutants out of the water, they do the same for the air. Trees are especially good at taking pollutants out of the air. And, of course, they give us oxygen! Wetlands and soil help to clean the air, too.

Biodiversity is also an important part of the carbon cycle. Carbon is a common natural element found in living and once-living things, as well as some non-living things. The carbon cycle is the process through which the element moves through the air, land, and water. Carbon in our air is in the form of a gas—carbon dioxide. Plants pull carbon dioxide from the air during photosynthesis. It is then passed to the animal that eats the plants and to the soil during decomposition.

DID YOU KNOW?

Carbon dioxide concentration in the air is the highest it has been in 800,000 years and it continues to rise.

Decomposers such as this fungus return nutrients to the soil, where the carbon cycle continues.
credit: Courtney Celley/USFWS (CC BY 2.0)

WORDS TO KNOW

drought: a long period of little or no rain.

mycorrhizal fungi: fungi that grow on the roots of plants to provide them with water and nutrients. These fungi also receive nutrients from the plants they grow on.

neuron: a special cell that sends electrical and chemical messages to your brain.

In the ocean, carbon dioxide is dissolved in the water. Marine plants use carbon in the same way plants on land do in photosynthesis. These processes on land and in the ocean store the carbon in living organisms or the soil, keeping it out of our atmosphere.

Nutrient cycling is another service that biodiversity provides. For plants to grow, they need healthy soil. In addition to sunlight, plants need nutrients from the soil. This is where the decomposers come in. They are responsible for breaking down dead organic matter, which returns nutrients to the soil, keeping it healthy.

Decomposition is the last step in the food chain—plants use the nutrients in the soil to grow, animals eat the plants and eat other animals, and at the end of the chain, decomposers return the nutrients to the soil.

DID YOU KNOW?

Coastal ecosystems such as mangrove swamps and salt marshes absorb and store carbon 50 times faster than areas the same size in a tropical rainforest.

Biodiversity performs many other ecosystem services. It helps reduce flooding. It controls erosion and regulates climate. It provides shelter for millions of other species. And biodiversity pollinates. Humans benefit from all these indirect services. As you will learn, we also benefit from the many direct services provided to us by biodiversity, such as food, shelter, and clothing.

ESSENTIAL QUESTION

Why is biodiversity so important?

Magnified Microbiome!

Wood Wide Web

Trees and plants communicate with each other using an internet made of fungus! When you walk through a forest, beneath your feet are miles and miles of complex, dense lines of communication among trees and plants. They use these lines to pass critical information and resources back and forth.

The fungi underground act as fiber-optic internet cables. They can transmit signals, or information, from one tree or plant to the next. They send information about insects, **drought**, and other dangerous factors. Older trees will even help young trees by sending them nutrients through the network. This "social" behavior of trees and plants ensures the survival of that population of the species. By looking out for each other, the community stays intact.

The lines are made of **mycorrhizal fungi**, which grow on the roots of trees and help protect them. These fungi also receive nutrients from the trees. These microscopically thin lines can grow to be 1,000 times the length of the tree roots. Because of that, the fungi can connect to other lines from other plants or trees. The threads of the fungi act like the **neurons** in our brains, sending signals back and forth.

CREATE A FOOD WEB

Food webs can help us understand how species in an ecosystem are connected. Let's take a closer look at food webs.

> **Find a yard or park or natural area near you.** Identify a single food chain in this space.

> **Write each item of the food chain on a separate notecard.** Start with the sun and then identify a plant that uses the sun's energy to grow.

> **Consider what organism obtains its energy by eating the plant.** Continue moving up the food chain. Go all the way up the food chain to the top predator.

> **Stay in the same spot but create a different chain.** Most likely some species will be part of more than one chain. Try to create five chains.

> **Time to create a web!** Spread out the notecards from the first chain, with the plants at the bottom and the final consumers at the top. Put arrows between the connected species.

> **Fit the next chain in with the first.** If a species is in the first chain, simply draw an arrow to it, connecting your chains. Do this for all the chains you discovered.

Consider This

Investigate each species in your web to determine other species they **prey** on as well as what preys on them. This will add connections to your web. You might also add other species that live in the space you observed that weren't in any of the food chains you documented. How do these other species fit into the overall web? What species are in the space that you can't see?

WORDS TO KNOW

prey: to hunt. Also animals hunted by other animals.

WHAT IF ALL THE SNAKES DISAPPEARED?

While some people like snakes, many do not, and would love to see snakes disappear. But, as you've learned, each species in an ecosystem plays an important role. If all the snakes went away, what would happen to the ecosystems in which they live?

❯ **Select a type of snake to study.** Gather information about its physical appearance, behavior, and ecosystem.

❯ **Consider the role the snake plays in that ecosystem.** This role could take on many forms—predator, prey, ecosystem engineer, or something else. You might also want to consider how snakes are important to people.

❯ **Once you've done this research, predict what would happen to their ecosystem if snakes disappeared.** How would other species and the habitat be affected? Keep in mind that the disappearance of snakes will have a "ripple effect" throughout the ecosystem—one change may cause another change that may then cause another.

❯ **Once you've made predictions, do an internet search** about "what would happen if snakes disappeared."

Consider This

Were your predictions correct? Were they complete or did you find more effects of a world without snakes than you'd predicted? Based on what you learned, can Earth do without snakes? Why or why not? Were these results surprising to you? Consider finding a way to visually represent your findings about the importance of snakes to educate others. This could be through a video, painting, slide show, or other media.

MAKE A WATER FILTER

Ideas for supplies: plastic disposable bottle, gravel, sand, cotton balls, dirty water, either natural or that you mix (water with visible particles is best)

One of the great ecosystem services provided by wetlands is water filtration. Without healthy, functioning wetlands, we would not have clean water. To get an idea of what goes into filtering water, make your own filter.

Caution: do not drink your "clean" water, even if it looks clear!

❯ **Start by cutting the bottle in half (have an adult help you).** Put the top part upside down inside the bottom part so the spout of the top will empty in the bottom part. You can also use a glass jar on the bottom to make the filter more stable. You will build the filter in the top half.

❯ **Put the filter materials in the top half by layering them.** Decide what order these materials should go in. Think about larger objects being filtered out first, then smaller particles. Once your filter is ready, pour the dirty water in.

❯ **Evaluate your filter.** How does the filtered water look when compared to the dirty water? Does it smell different? Feel different?

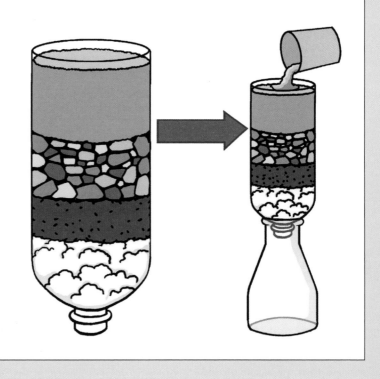

Clean Water for Everyone

There are many people on Earth who do not have access to clean water—more than 800 million! Water-related diseases lead to illness and even death. Innovators around the world are working to change this. One invention is called the Lifestraw. It is a straw about the width of a finger that filters water as it is pulled through it! In Cambodia, some communities have received ceramic water filters. The devices look like a clay version of a large Thermos water jug. Using the force of gravity, the tiny pores in the clay remove bacteria and other harmful organisms as water flows downward. Another idea uses the sun to purify water. The Life Sack is filled with water and put in the sun. The sun's rays heat and kill harmful microorganisms and make the water safe to drink. These and other inventive ideas are bringing safe, clean water to people who don't otherwise have access to it.

❯ **If your filter did not work as expected, consider what might have gone wrong and how you could improve the filter.** Brainstorm other materials you could use. What items make a good filter? Try the experiment again.

Consider This

Try looking at your dirty water through a high-powered microscope before you put it through your filter. Then, look at another sample after it goes through the filter. Do you see a difference? You could also research other ways to make water filters or how cities create their water filtration systems. You could even build your own mini-wetland in the top half of a plastic bottle.

CELEBRATE BIODIVERSITY!

In our busy, modern world, we don't often take the time to slow down and appreciate the biodiversity all around us and its importance to the health of the planet. This activity calls for you to do just that.

❯ **Your task is to create a piece of visual art that celebrates biodiversity.** It can celebrate biodiversity near you or around the world, unseen biodiversity, biodiversity at risk, or biodiversity in a single ecosystem. It's your choice!

❯ **Choose a medium to work with—painting, sculpture, collage, or something else.** The goal is to create a piece that allows you to focus on biodiversity and its value, and makes others stop to think.

❯ **You may want to start by visiting an art show or museum to get ideas for the type of piece you want to create.** Do some research on biodiversity to determine the focus of your piece. Now create!

Consider This

How did your artwork turn out? Was this easier or more difficult than you'd planned? Did the activity make you think more deeply about biodiversity on Earth? How could you share your piece with others? Consider posting it online, entering an art contest, or hanging it in your school. You could even gather a group of friends, have them create pieces as well, and put on an art show of your own to draw attention to biodiversity.

The murals on the walls of the London Zoo are meant to bring attention to the fate of rare and endangered species.

🔍 Louis Masai at London Zoo

This art show features the work of artists who celebrate the variety of biodiversity on Earth.

🔍 artists front line of biodiversity

Chapter 4

BIODIVERSITY AND
HUMANS

I GET THAT BIODIVERSITY IS IMPORTANT IN NATURE, BUT WE LIVE IN A CITY.

DOES IT REALLY AFFECT OUR LIVES ALL THAT MUCH?

LET'S SEE: YOU LIVE IN A HOUSE BUILT OF WOOD...

...AND YOU WEAR COTTON CLOTHES...

...AND YOU TAKE ASPIRIN WHEN YOU HAVE A HEADACHE...

...AND ANTI-BIOTICS WHEN YOU HAVE THE FLU.

ALL OF THOSE THINGS COME FROM BIODIVERSITY!

SO WITHOUT BIODIVERSITY I'D BE NAKED, COLD, AND SICK!

In the modern world, most humans are far removed from the natural world and biodiversity is often taken for granted. Biodiversity may also seem like something to simply study in school or hear about in the news.

But the truth is, biodiversity is everywhere, even in modern cities. Not only that, all humans are part of the web of life on Earth. All our food comes from nature. The ocean is a key source of protein for more than 3 billion people. Marine plants and algae provide more than 70 percent of the oxygen we breathe.

Humans depend on biodiversity just as much as any other species on the planet!

ESSENTIAL QUESTION

How is biodiversity important to humans?

FOOD

Let's start with breakfast. Think about what you ate this morning. Fruit? Milk? Eggs? Now, consider where those items came from. Fruit grows on trees or plants. Milk comes from cows. Chickens lay eggs. If you had a bowl of cereal, each of the ingredients for that cereal came from nature—the wheat, the nuts, the oats, and the sugar, too! Even highly processed foods are produced using ingredients found in nature.

The earliest humans were hunter gatherers. They hunted animals and they ate from the plants and trees around them. Later, our ancestors learned how to plant **crops** and raise animals in the ecosystem where they lived.

As time passed, people learned how to grow more food and became very efficient at producing enough to feed growing populations. While millions of people around the world still hunt or fish for their food, most of the food we eat today is produced by farmers and ranchers. But farmers and ranchers still rely on biodiversity to grow and maintain healthy crops. All of us rely on biodiversity for **food security**.

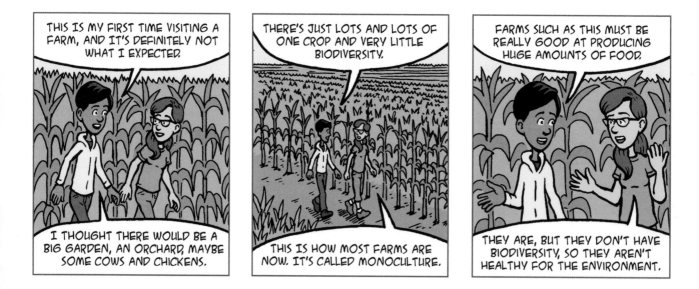

THIS IS MY FIRST TIME VISITING A FARM, AND IT'S DEFINITELY NOT WHAT I EXPECTED.

I THOUGHT THERE WOULD BE A BIG GARDEN, AN ORCHARD, MAYBE SOME COWS AND CHICKENS.

THERE'S JUST LOTS AND LOTS OF ONE CROP AND VERY LITTLE BIODIVERSITY.

THIS IS HOW MOST FARMS ARE NOW. IT'S CALLED MONOCULTURE.

FARMS SUCH AS THIS MUST BE REALLY GOOD AT PRODUCING HUGE AMOUNTS OF FOOD.

THEY ARE, BUT THEY DON'T HAVE BIODIVERSITY, SO THEY AREN'T HEALTHY FOR THE ENVIRONMENT.

Archaeological evidence suggests that rice farming began in Indochina more than 12,000 years ago.

To start, crops need healthy soil. To be healthy, soil needs a rich diversity of microorganisms. It also depends on decomposers to recycle nutrients. Burrowing organisms, such as termites and worms, help mix the layers of soil and the nutrients in it. The burrows these organisms make also increase the amount of moisture the soil can hold.

Insects also play a role in farming. We rely on bees and other pollinators to pollinate our crops. Some insects help us by eating the insects that harm crops. Ladybugs, for example, eat aphids and other pests. Ladybugs are such great pest predators that many farmers are now growing plants that attract these insects to their fields.

The problem is that many of today's large farms operate more like factories. Advances in science and technology allow farmers to plant and harvest one type of crop across their entire farms. For the farmers, this **monoculture** farming allows them to efficiently plant and harvest crops using machinery. These factory farms also tend to use a lot of harmful fertilizers and **pesticides**.

Healthy soil often has worms in it!
credit: Ron Nichols, USDA-NRCS

BIODIVERSITY

However, monoculture farming has proven to reduce local biodiversity and soil health. People are beginning to understand that farming practices need to change. Some farmers today promote greater biodiversity by planting a variety of crops. This diversity helps them to grow food that is less vulnerable to pests or disease or other environmental changes.

Planting a variety of different crops also promotes healthier biodiversity in the soil and supports nearby biodiversity. As you know, these interconnected ecosystems need each other to stay balanced and healthy.

DID YOU KNOW?

The oldest farmers on Earth are termites! They started farming fungus 25 million years ago.

Monoculture means only one crop, such as corn, is grown in an area.

credit: Nicholas A. Tonelli (CC BY 2.0)

Nature's Hidden Superpowers

Scientists know that nature has many superpowers, so they often look to nature for ideas. Giant sequoia trees, which grow to enormous heights and live for hundreds of years, are made of **nanofibers** of **cellulose**. These nanofibers are 10 times stronger than steel. Scientists are trying to reproduce what the sequoias do naturally to build stronger buildings.

Insects have superpowers, too. The cat flea can jump 100 times its height. If you could do that, you'd be able to jump to the top of the Statue of Liberty in a single leap. These fleas can do this because of an elastic material they produce that stretches and squishes and always snaps back. Imagine if you had that in your next pair of athletic shoes!

RESOURCES

In addition to food, biodiversity provides humans with **resources** we use for shelter, clothing, fuel, and more. Some of the natural resources we use are abiotic, such as water, the sun, gold, and silver. But many of the resources are biotic and depend on biodiversity.

Bizarre Biodiversity

Giant Sequoia: These hardy trees are not only among the tallest and widest trees on Earth, they are some of the oldest. Sequoia can grow to be more than 3,000 years old!

credit: Allie Caulfield (CC BY 2.0)

WORDS TO KNOW

fossil fuel: natural fuel that formed long ago from the remains of living organisms. Oil, natural gas, and coal are fossil fuels.

boll: the seed pod of the cotton plant that fluffy cotton fibers burst from.

Even today, many of our buildings and homes are constructed partly or entirely of wood from trees. We also use wood to build furniture and tools. Similarly, much of our clothing is made from plant fibers. Are you wearing a cotton T-shirt today? Or blue jeans? Cotton grows on a plant. Silk comes from the cocoons of silkworms. And wool is sheared off animals such as sheep and alpaca. Leather and fur come from animals, too.

How about fuel for cooking and heating? Long ago and in many rural communities today, that fuel comes from burning wood.

Even the **fossil fuels** that we rely on today to heat and cool our homes and to run our cars have their origin in biodiversity. Fossil fuels are the ancient buried remains of living organisms. Through millions of years, heat and pressure within the earth turned these fossils into oil, coal, and natural gas. They are considered biotic resources.

Cotton

Cotton is a soft, strong fabric used in about 40 percent of the clothing made in the world. Today, it is one of the leading agricultural crops, yet it has been around for thousands of years. Cotton begins as a small seed. After a few months, it grows

credit: Michael Bass-Deschenes (CC BY 2.0)

into a bushy plant that produces **bolls**. Inside these bolls are the soft fibers we think of when we think of cotton, as well as more cotton seeds. The soft fibers are harvested, processed, and spun, then woven into fabrics. However, there are environmental concerns about large-scale cotton production. As a crop, cotton requires a lot of water, and pesticides are used heavily on cotton plants. Plus, some countries that produce cotton rely on forced child labor.

Speaking of fossil fuel, can you spot any plastic from where you are sitting right now? Plastic is made from fossil fuel! Everything made of plastic had its origin in the earth's ancient biodiversity. Plastic is used to make all kinds of products—bottles, toys, pens, shopping bags, pens, phones, utensils, cups, and so much more. None of it would be possible if it hadn't been for the decayed plant and animals from long ago that created fossil fuels.

The next time you use a plastic bottle, think about the biodiversity that contributed to making it.

Countless other resources in your everyday life exist because of biodiversity. Many health and beauty products, as well as soap, are derived from nature. The books you read and the paper you write on were all made from trees. Perfumes, natural dyes, rubber, oils, and cork come from plants. When you use a bar of soap or a pen or an instrument or a ball, think about the biodiversity that made it possible!

WORDS TO KNOW

antibiotic: a medicine that can disable or kill bacteria.

Ebola: a disease caused by a virus that spreads easily; it causes severe internal bleeding and often death.

SARS: Severe Acute Respiratory Syndrome, a serious disease caused by a virus that spreads easily; it affects the lungs and breathing and can cause death.

malaria: a disease spread by infected mosquitoes. It is found mainly in the hot areas near the equator.

deforestation: the process through which forests are cleared to use land for other purposes.

HEALTH

In addition to providing humans with food, shelter, and clothing, biodiversity provides us with medicines. Native cultures have long used natural ingredients to cure illnesses, relieve pain, and heal wounds.

Did you know that dandelions aren't just weeds, but when eaten are a great source of vitamins A, B, C, and D? They have also been used to treat liver and digestive issues. Aloe, a cactus-like plant, produces a sticky gel often used to treat skin conditions such as burns and rashes. And the poppy plant is used for pain relief.

DID YOU KNOW?

Today's medicines use more than 70,000 different plant and tree species, but scientists have tested only 1 percent of species for their possible medicinal value.

Dandelions for dinner!

Bee Bacteria

The next time your doctor prescribes you an **antibiotic**, ask where it came from. It might have come from bee bacteria. People have used honey as a medicine for thousands of years because it is a natural antibiotic. Now, scientists are conducting further research into the bacteria in a bee's stomach. They have found that bee bacteria is a powerhouse at knocking down harmful bacteria. The bee bacteria can even knock down the superbugs that are becoming resistant to antibiotics. Perhaps one day, bee bacteria will replace many of the common medicines we use today.

Today, 50 percent of our modern medicines come directly or indirectly from nature.

These include cancer drugs, painkillers, heart medicines, and treatments for diabetes. One powerful drug for relieving severe pain comes from the venom of predatory cone snails. Scientists know more cures are out there, and continue to research plants, fungi, and bacteria around the world. Some medical research also involves studying animals or using other species for experimentation.

Biodiversity affects humans in numerous ways. Many of the effects come from the communities of microbes living in our bodies. And cavities?

Watch this video to find how biodiversity affects your teeth!

PBS gross cavities

Biodiversity loss, however, has led to an increase in the spread of infectious diseases. Deadly outbreaks of **Ebola**, **SARS**, avian flu, and **malaria** have been attributed to impacts on biodiversity. For example, clear-cutting forests reduces mosquito diversity. But for reasons unknown to scientists, the surviving species of mosquitoes are the ones that spread malaria. Plus, **deforestation** pushes infected mosquitoes and other diseased species into increased contact with humans.

GO PLAY OUTSIDE!

Biodiversity has social value as well. Have you been outdoors lately? Rowed a boat on a lake, taken a hike, or gone camping? Or maybe you went bird watching or saw a pair of squirrels chase each other around a tree. People love to visit natural places and enjoy the beauty. We are inspired by the natural world.

Magnified Microbiome!

Belly Buttons

Biodiversity exists not only around us, but also within us. Each person has more microbes inside them than there are people on Earth. That's more than 7 billion microbes! But before you get too grossed out, remember that microbes can be beneficial. They help to balance our human ecosystem. And, without all the beneficial microbes in and on your body, you would not survive—they are your first line of defense against harmful microbes!

Your belly button is one tiny habitat of your body. Recently, scientists have begun to explore that environment in much the same manner as explorers of a new world.

Rob Dunn is a biologist working at the Belly Button Biodiversity Project at North Carolina State University. The project was launched in 2011 to study the diversity of life found in belly buttons and to study how that diversity varies between people. They've found that the average belly button is home to dozens of different species of bacteria and other organisms! They have also discovered many species in belly buttons that science knows little about. Even more interestingly, the project has discovered whole new species!

DID YOU KNOW?

Stinky feet are caused by bacteria breaking down sweat!

The simple act of being in nature and watching nature makes people feel better. Research has shown that being outdoors benefits our physical and emotional well-being.

Outdoor recreation is an important part of tourism in many areas. This attracts visitors and brings in money. **Ecotourism** is now a growing industry.

Nature and its biodiversity also contribute to cultural identity.

Take a hike!
credit: Loren Kerns (CC BY 2.0)

In many cultures, songs, dances, and rituals are often centered around nature or a specific animal. Many of these cultures' religions and traditions are based on respect for the earth and its creatures. **Folklore** frequently includes animals and plants **native** to an area to symbolize that society's values. Even in the present day, in the United States, the bald eagle is a symbol for the country, representing strength and freedom.

For humans, biodiversity is invaluable. The **United Nations (UN)** estimates that nature is worth 30 times what the entire global economy is worth. That's a lot! However, calculating the value of nature is impossible. We use biodiversity in so many ways to sustain our lives. It is the foundation on which everything we have and everything we do rests. Yet this biodiversity that is so important is also at risk.

ESSENTIAL QUESTION

How is biodiversity important to humans?

BUILD A BIRD FEEDER

We find biodiversity even in our own backyards. Watching wildlife and enjoying nature can be relaxing. To bring biodiversity close, build a bird feeder to attract birds.

> **Begin by selecting a spot for the feeder that will keep the birds safe from predators.**

> **Consider what type of bird feeder you will make.** Research the different types of bird feeders that are possible. Write a list of the supplies you will need. If possible, make the feeder out of recycled materials—maybe use an empty half-gallon milk container or plastic bottle!

> **Investigate what kind of seeds** the native birds in your area prefer.

> **After you've finished, filled, and hung the bird feeder, take notes about the birds that visit.** You can use a bird guide to help you identify species you are unfamiliar with.

Consider This

How long did it take for birds to discover your feeder? Was it just one species at first? Which species was the most dominant? See if you can identify a pattern of behavior among one species or between species. In addition, pay attention to the time of day each species visits your feeder. Determine if some species are good at sharing with each other and if some are not so good at sharing. Also, were all the species that visited your feeder native to your area? Were there any **invasive species** of birds?

WORDS TO KNOW

invasive species: a species that is not native to an ecosystem and rapidly expands to crowd out and harm other species.

GROCERY STORE BIODIVERSITY

We live in a time when a wide variety of food is available to many people in grocery stores. But much of the food in stores travels long distances to get there. Let's take a look!

❯ Take a trip to the grocery store. Bring along your science journal and a pencil.

❯ At the store, observe the biodiversity in the produce section. Right away you should notice the species diversity—apples, oranges, carrots, lettuce, broccoli, and lots more.

❯ Now, look more closely. Is there a species that has more than one type? Perhaps the store is selling Gala, Honeycrisp, and Fuji apples. That is genetic diversity. Take note of the biodiversity you find.

❯ Make a chart like the one below to record your findings.

Species Diversity	Genetic Diversity			
Apples	Gala	Honeycrisp	Fuji	Granny Smith
Oranges				
Carrots				
Lettuce				
Broccoli				

Consider This

In the store, some species will have great genetic diversity—apples, for example. Why do you think that is? Which species had the greatest genetic diversity? Which had the least? Research how far some of that produce traveled to get to the grocery store so that customers had a wide array of biodiversity to choose from. You may want to take your investigation to other parts of the store. Try the dairy section or even the meat section.

CANDY BAR DISSECTION

Making candy bars is just one of the many ways humans use plant biodiversity for their own benefit. This delicious activity will help you to understand the biodiversity that goes into making a candy bar.

❯ Start with a trip into your pantry or to a nearby store to get a candy bar of your choice.

❯ Before you open it, look at the ingredients label on the candy bar. In your science journal, list the first five ingredients.

❯ Research the origins of each of those five ingredients. The almonds in your candy bar may have come from California (although the label most likely won't tell you), but almond trees are native to the Middle East. Investigate each of the ingredients this way.

❯ Record what you find in your science journal.

Consider This

Find a map or globe and mark on it where all the ingredients in your candy bar originated. Does this surprise you? Try looking at another candy bar to see if the ingredients are similar or different. You could even find a product labeled "made locally." Read the ingredients, then research whether they were all native to your area or not. Can you find a product that is truly native to your area? Once you are done with your research, it's time to enjoy that snack!

MAKE YOUR OWN MICROSCOPE

Supplies: laser pointer, smartphone, putty or clay, flashlight, small square of white paper, and two squares of stiff clear plastic (or microscope slides)

Without a microscope, we can't see a whole world of biodiversity. But if you have a microscope, you can discover some of the millions of microscopic organisms living all around you. Time to make one!

❯ **Begin by removing the small lens of the laser pointer.** You may need some tools to carefully dig it out.

❯ **Attach the lens to the camera on a smartphone using putty or clay, making sure that the rounded part of the lens is facing up.** Voila! You have a microscope. You can test it by looking at small text.

❯ **Set a flashlight on end with the light pointing up and turn it on.** Set the white paper over the light and the plastic or microscope slide on top of that. Find a sample of water from a puddle or stream or grab a pinch of dirt and add a tiny bit of water. Place your sample on the slide and place the second piece of plastic or slide on top.

❯ **Once your sample is set up, go to video mode on the phone and zoom in on your sample.** What do you see?

Consider This

How many different organisms can you see in one sample? Is this amazing to you or disgusting? Try taking samples from other places. Are the organisms you see similar or different? Now that you have a window into the microscopic world, what else can you investigate?

Chapter 5

THREATS TO
BIODIVERSITY

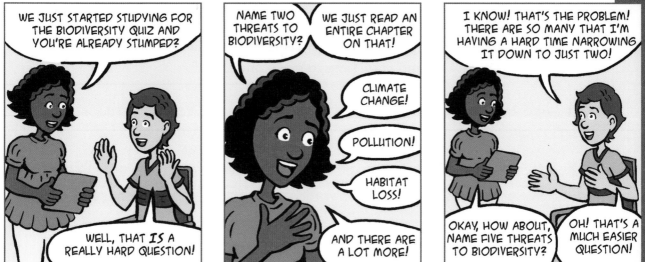

Throughout Earth's history, biodiversity has gradually increased. Yet as you know, at the same time, many species have gone extinct. No mastodons are lumbering down your street or pterodactyls are flying through the air. In fact, of the billions of species that have lived on the planet, 99 percent have gone extinct. It is a natural part of life on Earth.

Species become extinct for a number of reasons. Some are natural extinctions, called "background extinctions." These happen when species can't adapt to changes in their environment. The changes include habitat loss, the evolution of a new species, temperature or precipitation changes, or disease.

Other species have disappeared because of mass extinctions. These were natural events that happened suddenly, causing many species to die off in a short period of geologic time. There have been five mass extinctions in Earth's history.

ESSENTIAL QUESTION

What are the threats to biodiversity today?

Scientists warn that we are currently experiencing another mass extinction. No asteroids are headed our way, but conditions on Earth are changing so rapidly that some species cannot adapt. As a result, current extinction rates are 1,000 to 10,000 times higher today than the normal background rate of extinction. The cause? Humans.

Since the evolution of modern humans some 200,000 years ago, our population has swelled to more than 7 billion. As our numbers have grown, our species has transformed the earth to meet our needs. But with an ever-growing population, we have a greater and greater impact on the earth and on biodiversity.

A million years from now, what will the geologic record show about the impact of man? **Watch this TED-Ed video for a closer look at the ways the new age of mankind, the Anthropocene, will be part of the geologic record.**

(PS)

🔎 Ted-Ed human impacts

CLIMATE CHANGE

Climate change is often in the news. Scientists are very concerned about the effects climate change is having on the planet and its biodiversity. During the earth's 4.5-billion-year history, the climate has changed many times, from ice ages to periods when the earth's climate was mostly tropical. The problem today, though, is that the rate of climate change is too fast. And it's the result of human activity.

Bizarre Biodiversity

Seahorses: Unlike other species, the male seahorse, not the female, is responsible for the babies! He carries the developing embryos around in a pouch, much like that of a kangaroo.

greenhouse effect: when the presence in the atmosphere of gases such as carbon dioxide, water vapor, and methane allow incoming sunlight to pass through, but then trap that heat.

One cause of climate change is the burning of fossil fuels. People want energy to drive their cars and power transportation, heat and cool homes, produce electricity, and run factories. In our modern world, most of that energy comes from fossil fuels. However, these fuels emit gases as they are burned.

These gases, such as CO_2, work like a greenhouse, trapping heat in the earth's atmosphere— that's why it's called the greenhouse effect!

Deforestation is another cause of rising CO_2 levels in the atmosphere. Trees and plants naturally capture and store carbon. The removal of trees has reduced the amount of carbon being taken out of the atmosphere. Carbon dioxide levels in the atmosphere have varied over geologic time. Some CO_2 is necessary to keep our planet warm. However, today the levels are at an all-time high. Because of this, scientists predict that in the twenty-first century, the average temperature around the globe will rise between 2 and 5.2 degrees Fahrenheit (1.1 to 2.9 degrees Celsius).

This power plant at Apollo Beach, Florida, is releasing greenhouses gases into the atmosphere.

That rise in temperature may not seem like a lot—it might even sound nice to have warmer days. But think about it like this. You have on a hoodie and jeans and maybe a hat, too. You are comfortable—not too hot, not too cold. Then, someone cranks up the heat. Suddenly, you are sweating and shedding layers. Or you move to another room that's cooler. Or open a window to cool the room back down.

Polar bears depend on the ice because it serves as a platform from which to hunt for their favorite food—seals.
credit: Dr. Kathy Crane, NOAA Arctic Research Office

As a human, you are able to adapt quickly. Other species? Not so much. Trees in the rainforest of South America, for example, are gradually growing farther uphill to stay in a climate they are adapted to. But the change is happening too fast for them to keep up.

One impact of global warming is melting polar ice. The melting of sea ice will disrupt many polar species, including polar bears, which depend on the ice for hunting. In addition, as the ice melts, sea levels will rise, flooding many island and coastal habitats. These areas will simply be under water, putting all species in these locations at risk. Tigers are one species that stand to lose almost all of their breeding grounds as sea levels rise.

TED-Ed has put together an archive of short informational videos that can teach you more about our changing climate. **There are videos on renewable energy, the buildup of CO_2 in our atmosphere, animals' ability to adapt to climate change, human impacts in the geologic record, and more.**

(PS)

🔎 TED-Ed Changing Climate

WORDS TO KNOW

ocean acidification: the process by which the ocean absorbs carbon dioxide from the atmosphere, and through a series of chemical reactions, becomes more acidic.

coral bleaching: a sign of poor health in coral that happens when algae in the coral die or lose their color.

Climate change will also result in hotter temperatures, which threaten the survival of African wild dog pups, which are heat-sensitive. Rising temperatures mean shrinking water supplies, which affects many different species—including humans. Weather patterns are changing, too, causing more extreme weather events in many parts of the world.

Increased CO_2 levels affect marine life as well. The ocean naturally absorbs CO_2 from the atmosphere, where it dissolves. In the process, chemical reactions turn the CO_2 into an acid. But with more CO_2 in the atmosphere, more CO_2 is being absorbed by the oceans, and our oceans are becoming too acidic.

Coral bleaching at Mariana Islands, Guam
credit: David Burdick

Because of **ocean acidification**, many shelled marine species can't produce hard, healthy shells. Species such as clams, oysters, and mussels are threatened. Coral reefs are, too. Corals are actually animals that together form a community called a reef. Ocean acidification is causing coral growth to slow, and the corals' skeletons are weaker. Without healthy skeletons and shells, many species, including coral, are more vulnerable to predators and erosion.

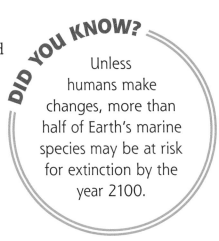

DID YOU KNOW?

Unless humans make changes, more than half of Earth's marine species may be at risk for extinction by the year 2100.

Coral reefs are also affected by higher water temperatures, which cause a loss of microscopic algae, the main food source of coral. This results in **coral bleaching**. The earth has already seen a steady decline in the number of healthy coral reefs. If coral reefs disappear, the many marine species that depend on coral reefs for food and shelter may disappear as well.

POLLUTION

When you think of pollution, what comes to mind? Perhaps you think of piles of litter along a street. Or a brown cloud spewing out of the smokestack of a factory. Or maybe an oil spill in the ocean. These are just a few examples of the many types of pollution that result from human activity. And each one affects biodiversity.

Pesticides in Honey

Bees are an extremely important part of the world's ecosystems. Not only do they pollinate flowers and crops, they also produce honey. Yet their numbers have been dropping significantly. This is partly due to climate change and habitat loss. Pesticides also affect bee populations. Scientists have even discovered traces of toxic pesticides in honey. When bees collect nectar from flowers or plants treated with chemicals, the pesticides go back to the hive with them.

WORDS TO KNOW

agriculture: growing plants and raising animals for food and other products.

runoff: produced when water picks up wastes as it flows over the surface of the ground. Runoff can pollute streams, lakes, rivers, and oceans.

single-use: describes an item that is made to be used only one time and then thrown away.

microplastic: a tiny piece of plastic less than 0.2 inch in size.

Pollution is any material or substance that comes into an environment and is poisonous or can cause harm. Similar to litter, smoke, and oil spills, many types of pollution are easy to see. But many serious pollution threats to biodiversity cannot be seen.

The fertilizers and pesticides used in **agriculture** are one threat that is gaining more attention. Pesticides do a great job of getting rid of pests, but they also kill other insects as well as beneficial microbes in the soil. Then, the harmful chemicals make their way into the soil and the water, affecting fish and other organisms.

An algae bloom
credit: Eric Vance, U.S. EPA

And while some fertilizers and animal waste are not directly toxic, they are full of nutrients that upset the balance of nearby and downstream habitats. Nitrogen fertilizers have caused many "dead zones" in the earth's oceans and other water sources.

A dead zone is an area where nitrogen has created an overgrowth of algae—an algae bloom. Some of the algal blooms are toxic, killing fish and marine birds and mammals. Whether directly toxic or not, when the algae die and decompose, the process takes up all the oxygen in the surrounding water. With little or no oxygen, most marine life cannot survive.

A beach in Hawaii covered in plastic debris.
credit: U.S. Fish and Wildlife Service Headquarters (CC BY 2.0)

The earth's oceans have growing numbers of dead zones. One of the largest forms every spring along the Gulf of Mexico in the southern United States as a result of fertilizer **runoff** from farms far upstream in the Missouri and Mississippi watersheds.

Another source of pollution that goes unnoticed, especially in the ocean, is plastic trash.

Plastic has become a big part of our lives. Much of the plastic produced, however, is **single-use** plastic. That means you use it once and throw it away—think of plastic bottles, bags, and utensils. Unfortunately, only a small percentage of plastic gets recycled. The rest ends up in landfills or makes its way into the ocean. Even worse, plastic never decomposes. As time passes, it does break down into smaller and smaller pieces, called **microplastics**, but it never fully goes away. This has become an enormous problem for marine life. The problem is so bad that huge garbage patches have formed in the world's oceans. These patches are places where ocean currents bring the trash together in gigantic swirls that cover millions of square miles.

Does this look like a jellyfish to you? It does to a sea turtle!

credit: Ben Mierement, NOAA NOS (ret.)

DID YOU KNOW?

Every year, approximately 9 million tons of plastic trash go into the ocean.

The issue of plastic trash in the ocean affects more than 700 marine species. Some species get tangled in discarded fishing nets. Others, such as sea turtles, eat the plastic by accident. Unfortunately, a plastic bag floating in the ocean looks a lot like a jellyfish—the turtles' favorite food.

The Laysan albatross on Midway Atoll in the North Pacific also mistakes plastic trash for food. Sadly, they bring this plastic "food" back to their young. On the atoll, the stomachs of dead birds are found to be full of plastic trash.

Plastic trash in our oceans is one of the greatest threats facing biodiversity in the sea. And plastic bottles are one of the leading sources of this trash. Every minute, 1 million of these bottles are bought around the world.

 But less than 10 percent are recycled. **Learn about the origin of these bottles and what happens when they aren't disposed of properly.**

🔎 Ted ed plastic bryce

The birds starve to death with a full stomach.

Plastic pollution affects the entire food chain. Even if an organism ingests plastic and isn't harmed right away, the plastic itself is toxic. The toxins have effects on a species' reproduction, health, and survival skills. Then, when another species comes along and eats the first, they are taking in microplastics and toxic chemicals, too. This happens all the way up the food chain to humans. A study by a university in Belgium found that people who eat seafood regularly eat up to 11,000 bits of microplastic per year!

HABITAT LOSS AND FRAGMENTATION

As the human population grows, more and more of the earth's land surface is converted for human use. Some of this is for development—houses, grocery stores, cities, roads, and more. Much of it is for agricultural uses to feed growing populations.

Every time land is converted for human use, other species are killed or pushed out. Can you imagine a bear knocking on your door and saying, "Hey, get out. Time to move on." The bear moves into the kitchen, mountain lions make dens in the basement, and birds take over the attic. And you are out of a home.

Garbage Patches

In the world's oceans, there are five large swirling masses of trash called garbage patches. How does this happen? Most of the trash originates on land and makes its way into the sea. Sometimes, cargo ships lose their loads, which dumps more debris into the ocean. The debris is then caught up in ocean currents. Where these currents meet, the water swirls in a gigantic spiral, concentrating the debris in one place. These garbage patches are not solid islands of plastic, but places in the ocean where the trash is concentrated. It's like a thin soup with flakes of plastic and the occasional larger chunks of plastic. The largest patch is the Great Pacific Garbage Patch. It is estimated to be more than twice the size of Texas.

WORDS TO KNOW

fragmentation: the act of breaking something into smaller sections or pieces.

over-exploitation: the hunting or taking of a natural resource (such as animals or trees) faster than the population can reproduce, which often leads to extinction.

poaching: the illegal hunting and killing of animals.

medicinal: having properties that can be used to treat illnesses.

When species lose their habitat, they must adapt or move.

Otherwise, they will die. Think about what might have lived on the very spot your home or school is on now. What was the native habitat?

Habitat destruction has become the leading cause of biodiversity loss around the world. Can you imagine a world without orangutans in the wild? That's exactly what is happening. Orangutans are on the brink of extinction because their habitat in Indonesia and Malaysia is being cleared for palm oil production and other agricultural uses. This type of deforestation is occurring around the world, including in the old-growth forest of the Pacific Northwest. The deforestation results in the loss of tree species as well as the plants and animals in that ecosystem.

DID YOU KNOW?

Humans have converted 37 percent of Earth's land surface to agricultural uses.

An orangutan in Indonesia
credit: Tim Laman (CC BY 4.0)

As humans continue to convert land, we divide natural ecosystems into smaller and smaller pieces. This **fragmentation** restricts species to living in smaller areas. The fragments are cut off from other fragments and may not provide species with enough space to roam, eat, and find a mate.

OVER-EXPLOITATION

Another threat to biodiversity is **over-exploitation**. Humans are hunting some species faster than those species can reproduce.

Illegal wildlife trade is a type of over-exploitation that occurs around the world. Also called **poaching**, this occurs when animals are hunted or captured even though they are protected.

An adult pangolin with a baby
credit: U.S. Fish and Wildlife Service Headquarters (CC BY 2.0)

Pangolins, a scaly anteater, are one of these animals. They are killed for their scales. In China and Vietnam, it is believed that these scales have **medicinal** value.

Similarly, sharks are killed for their fins to make shark-fin soup in Asia. The demand for shark fins is so great that many shark species are at risk for extinction, and as many as 100 million sharks are killed each year. Elephants are killed for their ivory tusks, rhinos for their horns, and tigers for their fur.

People who keep track of elephant populations noted a 30-percent decline in African elephants between 2007 and 2014. The fear is that if the poaching continues at that rate, these elephants will be extinct by the year 2040.

Over-exploitation affects many other species as well. People trade exotic birds as pets. Plants are illegally traded, too. People commit these crimes because the demand is huge and the money is good. Yet this wildlife trade is considered one of the greatest threats to endangered species.

Even common species with large populations can quickly suffer from over-exploitation.

Bizarre Biodiversity

Red Crab: This land crab that lives only on islands in the Indian Ocean migrates in masses (about 15 million!) from the forest to the ocean.

credit: DIAC images (CC BY 2.0)

The ocean, for example, was once thought to hold a never-ending supply of fish. Off the coast of Newfoundland, Canada, people made their living fishing for cod for more than 500 years. But as technology improved and human populations grew, larger and larger catches were harvested.

By 1992, the cod population was only 1 percent of what it was in the 1980s. To try to fix the situation, all cod fishing was banned. More than 20 years later, the population had recovered a little, but was still only 25 percent of 1980s levels. Many species have gone extinct due to this type of over-exploitation, including the passenger pigeon, the Steller's sea cow, and the Pinta Island tortoise.

DID YOU KNOW?

Noise and light pollution are also affecting species, including birds, sea turtles, and whales.

Magnified Microbiome!

Indoors

Humans have explored ecosystems around the planet, but ones that we still don't know much about are the ecosystems within our own homes!

Microbes are everywhere indoors—on doorknobs, floors, light switches, toilet seats, counters, sinks, your pillow, and more. Even the air is full of microbes. One cubic meter of indoor air has up to 10 million cells of bacteria! But as you've learned, most of these microbes are not bad. These helpful microbes are needed to maintain healthy environments.

Researchers have discovered that humans have a complicated relationship with the microbes in our homes. Home microbiome studies are looking into these organisms we share our homes with to understand the role they have in human health. And while the microbes affect us humans, the research has already found that the people living within a home affect the microbes there. When someone leaves a house for a few days, taking their microbes with them, the microbe community in the home changes.

INVASIVE SPECIES

Invasive species can threaten biodiversity, too. Sometimes, humans bring species from one place to another, either accidentally or on purpose. Species introduced from somewhere else don't always cause harm to an ecosystem. However, when an introduced species upsets an ecosystem's balance and decreases ecosystem function, it is considered invasive.

This happens when the new species finds itself in an ecosystem with few predators. It might do well against native species in the competition for food and other resources. It might also reproduce quickly. Often, native species have no defenses, can't escape, or cannot adapt. The result is that the entire food web is altered and ecosystem function decreases.

Zebra mussels on a native mussel
credit: U.S. Fish and Wildlife Service

Ever since humans began to travel the globe, species of plants, animals, bacteria, and other organisms have traveled with them. The zebra mussel is a species native to Russia that made its way to the United States as a hitchhiker on the hulls of ships. First discovered in the United States in 1982, the tiny zebra mussel is causing great problems for the ecosystems of the Great Lakes and rivers of the country. They attach themselves to and damage native mussels, filter out algae that native species use for food, and gum up any water filtrations or intake systems on the river or lake.

DID YOU KNOW?

The brown tree snake was accidentally introduced to the island of Guam at the end of World War II and has since wiped out the native bird population.

Another type of invasive species that is proving to be especially deadly is disease. Again, species evolve and adapt to their environment through time. But when a new disease is introduced, species do not have the defenses to fight the disease.

One example is the chytrid fungus that affects amphibians. Humans have helped spread the fungus around the world through the wildlife trade, causing one of the largest wildlife extinctions ever seen. The fungus is responsible for extinction of hundreds of species of frogs and other amphibians.

More than any other species that has come before us, humans have had an enormous impact on Earth and on biodiversity. Technology has increased our ability to transform the planet to meet our needs. And as the human population continues to grow, so does our impact.

In fact, as the human population increases, species diversity decreases.

By the year 2050, the human population on Earth is expected to reach 9 billion. Meanwhile, more than 23,000 species around the world are at risk for extinction. That includes more than 40 percent of all amphibians, 33 percent of reef-building corals, and 13 percent of birds. The question becomes, what can we do about it?

ESSENTIAL QUESTION

What are the threats to biodiversity today?

WANTS VS. NEEDS

In the modern world, we tend to use the word "need" quite a bit. But as a species, how much do we truly need? Let's take a look.

❯ **Create a two-column table.** Label the first column "needs" and the second column "wants."

❯ **Begin by considering what you think the definition of "need" is.** What is the definition of "want" in comparison?

❯ **Now, think carefully about what you, as a human, need for basic survival.** List these things that you absolutely cannot live without. If you are being honest, this "needs" column will have only four or five items.

❯ **Now, list things in your life** that you want in the "wants" column.

❯ **As you look at your list, do you think that the needs of all humans are the same?** How about the wants? Was there a time when your needs were not met? What did you do? How do humans respond when their needs aren't met?

❯ **Compare your list** with lists made by family, friends, or classmates.

Consider This

Now, consider plants and animals in nature. What do they need to survive? Do different species have different needs? Are other species' needs different from yours? How do humans' wants interfere with the needs of other species?

OIL SPILL

When humans drill for and transport oil, sometimes oil spills in the ocean. When these disasters happen, millions of gallons of oil are released into the sea, affecting all biodiversity. Birds are some of the many victims. Start a scientific method worksheet and predict how you think birds' feathers might be affected by an oil spill and how that, in turn, might affect the bird.

Caution: Wear gloves to handle the feathers.

❯ **To understand how oil affects birds' feathers,** find some loose feathers and clean them.

❯ **Put some oil, such as olive oil or bike oil, on the feathers and rub it in.** Then, drop water on the feathers. What happens? How would a bird be affected if all its feathers were coated in oil? What would happen to the bird?

❯ **Try to clean the oil off the feathers.** What happens if you use cold water? Hot water? Try adding dish soap to the water—does that help? What else can you try? What does this tell you about the difficulty of cleaning up large oil spills in the ocean?

DID YOU KNOW?

After oil spills, countless volunteers turn out to rescue affected birds. They use Dawn dishwashing liquid to remove the oil from birds' feathers!

Consider This

Investigate further to learn how oil spills affect birds to see if your prediction was correct. Then, research recent oil spills to learn how the entire ecosystem was affected. Does the ecosystem recover? How long might that take? Can you come up with some creative solutions to help birds after an oil spill? Use your feathers to investigate solutions.

ACID RAIN

Ideas for supplies: pots, soil, plant seeds, vinegar

Acid rain is one of the many problems resulting from pollution in the air. Acid rain forms when water vapor combines with chemicals in the air from burning coal and fossil fuels, from manufacturing, or from other smoke. The precipitation falls as acid rain. Start a scientific method worksheet. What do you predict that the effects of acid rain might be on biodiversity?

> **Label three pots as #1, #2, and #3.** Plant the same type of seeds in each pot. Use fast-growing seeds such as beans or peas. Use the same type of soil for each pot as well.

> **Water plant #1 with 100-percent water.** Give plant #2 a mix of about 90-percent water and 10-percent vinegar. Finally, water plant #3 with a 50-50 mix of water and vinegar.

> **Which plant do you think will grow the fastest?** Which will be the healthiest? Make your predictions and record them in your science journal. Make observations every day and take notes in your science journal.

DID YOU KNOW?

American wildlife ecologist and author Aldo Leopold (1887–1948) once noted, "We abuse land because we regard it as a commodity belonging to us. When we see land as a community to which we belong, we may begin to use it with love and respect."

Consider This

Were your predictions correct? How was the growth of each plant similar? How were they different? Now think about plants in nature. How are they affected by acid rain? Can they adapt to this change? Consider the rest of the food chain. How might other species be affected by acid rain? How might ecosystems be affected? How does acid rain affect humans?

WORDS TO KNOW

acid rain: precipitation that has been polluted by acid.

Chapter 6

PROTECTING
BIODIVERSITY

According to studies, scientists estimate that three out of four species will go extinct in the next 300 years. Yet these same scientists know that humans have the tools to slow, stop, and even reverse this trend. Now is the time to focus our efforts on protecting biodiversity at the individual, community, national, and global levels.

ESSENTIAL QUESTION

What can we do to protect biodiversity on Earth?

Researcher and biologist E.O. Wilson said, "Destroying rainforest for economic gain is like burning a Renaissance painting to cook a meal." Let's look at some ways humans can avoid burning a priceless work of art—or a planet!

WORDS TO KNOW

crustacean: a group of marine animals that includes crabs, lobsters, shrimps, and barnacles.

LAWS, TREATIES, AND POLICIES

One way to protect biodiversity is to pass laws. Local laws are a first step. Local policies can establish recycling programs, community gardens, parks, cleanups, and more. At a higher level, national laws can help protect biodiversity within a country. In the United States, one of the best examples of this is the Endangered Species Act (ESA). This act was passed by the U.S. Congress in 1973, when people started to understand the value of biodiversity and to recognize the threats to biodiversity.

The ESA created a program to help protect and recover endangered birds, insects, fish, reptiles, mammals, **crustaceans**, flowers, grasses, and trees. It became illegal "to harass, harm, pursue, hunt, shoot, wound, kill, trap, capture, or collect" these species. The act also protects and monitors the habitats where these species are found.

As of 2017, there were more than 1,300 protected species in the United States!

The U.S. Fish and Wildlife Service protects species such as the California least terns by posting signs around their habitat to warn people to leave the birds alone.

credit: Pacific Southwest Region USFWS

AREA CLOSED
To protect nesting birds

Ventura Audubon Society

California Least Tern Nesting Area

The endangered California least tern uses this area for courtship and nesting from April 1st through September 15th each year. Disturbance by humans or their pets will cause parents to leave their nests or young, which may result in death of eggs or chicks due to exposure.

Please help us protect this nesting colony by avoiding this area.

These birds and their habitat are PROTECTED under the Endangered Species Act of 1973, and California Department of Fish and Game Code Sections 12002 and 12008.

Report Disturbances to: 1-888-DFG-CALTIP (1-888-334-2258)

credit: Miguel Vieira (CC BY 2.0)

The American alligator is a species that has been protected by law for more than half a century. Prior to the protection that it first received in the 1960s, the number of alligators had declined to the point they were in danger of extinction. Not only were the alligators hunted for their skins, but the habitats where they lived in the southeastern part of the United States were being destroyed. Once they were protected by a 1967 law and later by the ESA, alligator numbers increased. By 1987, the American alligator population had fully recovered. While the alligators are no longer endangered, they remain listed as "threatened" and they are still protected.

However, wild species don't know or care about the boundaries between countries—they are free to move back and forth across national borders. A bald eagle, for example, doesn't spread the word among fellow eagles to avoid crossing into Mexico, where pesticide use is not as well-regulated and monitored as it is in the United States. Plus, as you've learned, biodiversity loss in one area can affect biodiversity in another.

WORDS TO KNOW

treaty: a formal agreement between two or more countries.

convention: an agreement among countries.

conservation: managing and protecting natural resources.

That's why international cooperation is important, too. Once people started to understand how interconnected our world is, international laws and **treaties** were enacted so that countries could work together. One such agreement, the **Convention** on International Trade in Endangered Species (CITES), was signed in 1975. This agreement bans the international trade of endangered species to prevent their extinction.

DID YOU KNOW?

May 22 is International Day for Biological Diversity. It was initiated in 1993 to bring awareness of biodiversity and the issues facing it.

Learn More

To learn more about a few of the many international efforts to protect biodiversity, visit these sites.

The Sustainable Ocean Initiative is dedicated to finding a balance between sustainable use and conservation.

The Convention on Biological Diversity promotes the sustainable use and conservation of biodiversity.

The Ramsar Convention is an international treaty that guides wetland use and conservation.

The Intergovernmental Panel on Climate Change provides scientific evidence to influence global leaders' policies regarding climate change.

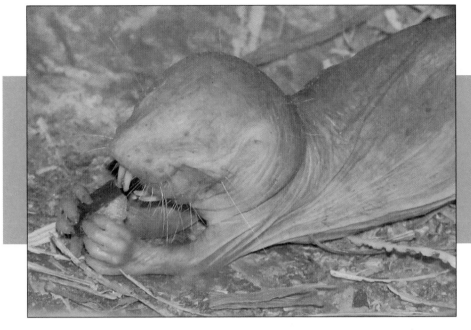

Bizarre Biodiversity

Naked mole rat: This hairless rodent lives its life underground in a complex network of burrows in east Africa.

Another example of international cooperation to protect biodiversity took place at the United Nations in 2015. Leaders from about 193 countries adopted the Sustainable Development Goals. One of the three major goals of this agreement was a commitment to combat climate change. These goals also called for finding a balance between human need and protecting the planet. All these international laws, treaties, and policies create a global community of advocates working together to preserve biodiversity.

CONSERVATION EFFORTS

In addition to laws, policies, and treaties, **conservation** efforts are taking place around the world to protect biodiversity. Some of these conservation efforts are run by governments, while others are run by private and nonprofit organizations or by individuals. These organizations influence environmental policy, support stronger laws to protect biodiversity, work on the ground to help individual species, push for more protected areas, and more.

Theodore Roosevelt and John Muir

One of the first environmental groups in the United States was the Sierra Club. It was founded by naturalist John Muir (1838–1914) in 1892, and today is one of the most powerful conservation organizations in the United States. In its history, the Sierra Club has played a role in protecting millions of acres of wilderness and in the passage of numerous environmental laws.

The Sierra Club has been involved in establishing many of the U.S. national parks. The park system is run by the U.S. government and today there are 58 national parks in the country and many other national monuments, lakeshores, and seashores. This system protects more than 84 million acres and provides educational experiences for more than 300 million visitors each year.

Other organizations work on the international level, including the United Nations Educational, Scientific and Cultural Organization (UNESCO). Its goal is to identify, protect, and preserve important cultural and natural sites.

Conservation Organizations

Dozens of conservation groups around the world are dedicated to protecting biodiversity. Spend some time learning about the work of these organizations.

› The Nature Conservancy

› Environmental Defense Fund

› World Wildlife Fund

› Natural Resources Defense Council

› National Audubon Society

› Conservation International

› Greenpeace

› Ocean Conservancy

DID YOU KNOW?

Worldwide there are more than 15,600 marine protected areas. They cover an estimated 9.7 million square miles of ocean.

One of the most well-known UNESCO natural sites is the Great Barrier Reef off the northeast coast of Australia. The world's largest collection of reefs is an ecosystem supporting 1,500 species of fish.

Marine protected areas (MPAs) are also important to preserving biodiversity. These areas are set aside to be protected and managed, just as a national park would be. This includes conserving the whole ecosystem and protecting the species that live there.

Want to know how much of the planet is protected? **Use this interactive map to explore all the places on Earth that have been designated as protected areas.** You can zoom in on the map and click on areas to learn their names or type the name of an area that interests you.

(PS)

🔎 protected planet

WORDS TO KNOW

sustainable: designed to minimize environmental impact.

biofuel: a fuel made from living matter, such as plants.

renewable energy: power that comes from sources that will never run out, such as the sun and wind.

turbine: a machine with blades turned by the force of water, air, or steam.

In the United States, MPAs are on every coast, as well as in the Great Lakes region. Internationally, the number of MPAs continues to grow. In 2018, Seychelles created two new protected areas in the Indian Ocean that will preserve an area the size of Great Britain.

While many protections are in place for ecosystems around the world, work still remains to be done. As of 2015, only about 15 percent of the land on Earth was protected, and less than 10 percent of our oceans were protected. Some experts assert that we must protect 50 percent of the planet to preserve biodiversity, ecosystem stability, and a healthy Earth.

THE ROLE OF SCIENCE

Science plays an important role in protecting biodiversity. Research helps us to better understand how we impact our world. It also helps us to create ways to live **sustainably** and protect biodiversity on land and in the water.

New buildings are designed to use less energy and create less pollution. Artificial wood was invented to use instead of trees—some of it is even made using recycled plastic!

Nets-to-Energy

Countless scientists and researchers around the world are exploring alternatives to fossil fuel. One program in Hawaii has not only found an alternative, but the alternative helps to clean up the ocean and shorelines. The Nets-to-Energy program collects discarded fishing nets, which are one of the leading types of marine debris. The nets are transported to a recycling facility where they are chopped into small bits. At another facility, the bits are burned. The steam produced drives a turbine that generates electricity. Since 2002, this program has used more than 800 tons of nets to create electricity.

Wind turbines harness the power of wind.

Cities are promoting alternative transportation. Researchers are exploring new ways to power cars, including the use of **biofuel** as an alternative to gasoline. Electric cars are becoming more affordable and more popular.

Scientists are also exploring ways to generate **renewable energy** to reduce or stop the use of fossil fuels.

One renewable source of energy is the wind. This technology uses **turbines** to collect the wind's power. When the wind blows, it turns the blades of large, windmill-like towers. The turning blades create energy. Solar panels offer the potential to provide us with another source of renewable energy. When homes and businesses use solar panels, they capture the energy from the sun to generate electricity.

hydroelectric: energy from moving water converted to electricity.

innovation: a new invention or way of doing something.

captive breeding: the process of mating wild animals to produce and raise offspring in places such as zoos, aquariums, reserves, and other conservation facilities.

Perhaps one of the oldest forms of renewable energy is **hydroelectric** power. For thousands of years, people have used moving water to help them with their work. Today, water is used to generate electricity. As water flows through dams, it turns blades on a turbine, which generates power.

Energy from ocean waves is being explored. And, unlike the sun and the wind that come and go, waves never stop!

Scientific research is guiding sustainable farming practices.

This includes understanding the biodiversity in the soil itself, which promotes healthier crops. Now, many farmers are deciding against using pesticides and chemical fertilizers that destroy biodiversity. They are choosing practices that support it.

Seaweed Farming

Ocean farming is a new type of farming that is gaining popularity. This innovative type of farming uses acres of ocean to plant crops three-dimensionally—in rows across the surface and in columns going down into the water. Sugar kelp, a type of seaweed, is one of those crops. The best part? It doesn't need fertilizer. And it doesn't need to be watered. This mild-tasting seaweed is making its way onto more and more menus, and can also be used as animal feed and fertilizer. Even more importantly, these marine plants help to clean up the ocean. Like all other plants, kelp can help absorb some of the carbon dioxide in the oceans.

An important **innovation** that draws from traditional farming methods is to plant a variety of crops in an area. It promotes biodiversity and at the same time can also increase crop production and natural resistance to pests.

Other scientists are concerned with directly conserving species. **Captive breeding** programs can help to bring species back from near extinction. Scientists in California have also created a Frozen Zoo. After collecting DNA samples from living species, the samples are brought to the zoo and frozen. The hope is to preserve life before it disappears so that maybe one day, scientists will be able to bring the extinct species back to life.

For plants, scientists have established seed banks. They are collecting and storing billions of seeds from all over the world.

Inside the Svalbard Global Seed Vault
credit: Dag Endresen (CC BY 3.0)

If done right, these seeds will still be able to germinate in hundreds, if not thousands, of years.

All this scientific research and experimentation guides world leaders. Armed with the best scientific information, leaders can make well-informed decisions about how to protect Earth's biodiversity.

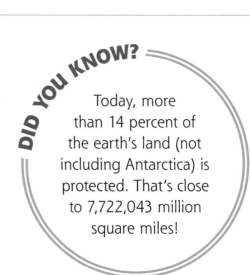

DID YOU KNOW?

Today, more than 14 percent of the earth's land (not including Antarctica) is protected. That's close to 7,722,043 million square miles!

THINK GLOBALLY, ACT LOCALLY

"Think globally, act locally" is a saying that is a call to action. If all of us help to preserve biodiversity in our communities, the whole planet will benefit. You might wonder how something such as recycling one plastic bottle or plastic bag can help save biodiversity. You are just one person after all! But think about what might happen if that bag isn't disposed of properly and ends up in the ocean. Consider the sea turtle swimming around looking for a tasty jellyfish.

Poachers Become Protectors

In Namibia, a small African country, poaching was a way of life in poor, rural areas. Yet around 1980, people recognized that wildlife was disappearing. An organization called the Integrated Rural Development and Nature Conservation approached the local communities. It proposed a radical idea—what if poachers were paid to look after the wildlife instead of killing it? Through this program, locals reclaimed their land and their connection to nature, and the wildlife populations rebounded. Now, these communities rely on conservation and tourism as the basis of their economy, which is founded on a renewed respect for biodiversity.

Things You Can Do

You can help to protect biodiversity in many ways right from your own home and community. Here are a few ideas.

1. Reduce, reuse, recycle.

2. Walk or bike as often as possible.

3. Save energy—turn off items that use electricity when not in use and use energy-efficient light bulbs and appliances in your home.

4. Eat local, sustainably farmed and harvested food.

5. Stop using single-use plastics such as bags, bottles, and utensils.

6. Be a smart shopper—don't buy items that harm biodiversity or ecosystems.

7. Educate someone else.

Even more importantly, do some math. Let's say you stop using plastic bottles completely and use a reusable water bottle instead. If you use it every day of the week for school, that's five plastic bottles saved. Multiply that by every day of the school year, and that's about 180 bottles saved. Now, what would happen if you convinced everyone in your family to do the same? And everyone in your class. It adds up!

Bizarre Biodiversity

Monkey Cup: This is a carnivorous type of pitcher plant. It lures insects into the pitcher with attractive odors. Once inside, the insect cannot grip the sides and falls into the water below.

credit: Richard W Sinyem (CC BY 2.0)

Potholes

Have you ever noticed small pools of water collected in a depression in a rock? These pools, called potholes, are their own mini-ecosystems! The rock pools can vary in size. Some of them hold water all the time, while others have water only part of the time. Some species of animals and insects use the pools only when they are full and other species live there permanently.

Each organism found in these pools is uniquely adapted to surviving in that environment. Some can burrow into the fine sediment at the bottom of the pool—their **exoskeleton** is waterproof and prevents them from **dehydrating**. Another adaptation of pothole species is a short lifespan. This ensures that the species reaches adulthood quickly in an environment where the water may not stick around very long. Other species lay eggs that do not hatch all at the same time, so at least one set of eggs survives to adulthood.

Probably one of the most fascinating adaptations is the ability of a species to lose up to 92 percent of the water in its body and still survive. This adaptation, called **cryptobiosis**, is generally one phase of the organism's life cycle.

credit: James St. John

All these adaptations are critical to the survival of a species in these mini-ecosystems. Yet subtle changes in the habitat can destroy it. These changes can be caused by pollution, climate change, and human contact. Even putting your hand in one of these pools can alter the environment.

DID YOU KNOW?

American author Edward Everett Hale (1822–1909) said, "I am only one, but I am one. I cannot do everything, but I can do something. And I will not let what I cannot do interfere with what I can do."

The bottom line is that the choices we all make every day affect biodiversity, both directly and indirectly. The key is education. Sometimes, people simply don't know how individual choices can have global impacts. If people were to stop buying items made of ivory, for example, poachers would no longer kill elephants. The same goes for animal furs. If there is no demand for a product, the trade will stop.

WORDS TO KNOW

exoskeleton: a skeleton on the outside of a body.

dehydrate: to take the water out of something.

cryptobiosis: a temporary state in which an organism's bodily process slows or stops under extreme conditions.

food miles: how far food travels from farm to table.

emission: something sent or given off, such as smoke, gas, heat, or light.

carbon footprint: the total amount of carbon dioxide and other greenhouse gases emitted over the full life cycle of a product or service, or by a person or family in a year.

Even the food we eat has an impact on the environment. Consider eating only fish that is sustainably harvested to protect fish populations. Or focus on eating food that is grown locally, which reduces **food miles** and cuts down on carbon **emissions**. Avoiding meat or eating less meat is important, too! The meat industry has a large **carbon footprint**—greater than the transportation industry!

To help you make informed choices about the seafood you eat, use the Monterey Bay Aquarium's website or app.

seafood watch

It's important that all of us make informed decisions in our everyday lives. We are living in a critical time. Right now, humans are at a crossroads. We understand our impact on biodiversity and our connection to it. And we have the intelligence and technology to make positive changes. But these changes will require a massive shift in how all of us think, live, and act. Can we make these changes, as individuals and as part of the human race?

ESSENTIAL QUESTION

What can we do to protect biodiversity on Earth?

GO ON AN ENERGY DIET

We use fossil fuels to heat and cool our homes, for electricity, food production, transportation, and more. Yet burning fossil fuels contributes to global warming. To slow, stop, and reverse this trend, all of us need to cut our use of fossil fuels. If we all do it, we could make a big difference!

❯ **Go on an energy diet for a week.** Begin by making a list of the ways you use energy—in the home, moving around town, and in what you buy at the store.

❯ **Critically examine the list to determine ways you can cut your energy use.** You may want to investigate on the internet to discover even more ways we use energy and how to cut its use.

❯ **Make a plan for how you will cut your energy use for a week and record your plan in your science journal.** What will you have to stop doing? What will you do instead? How else will using less energy affect your life?

Consider This

Have an adult help you to identify how much electricity your home uses in a week, on average, before you begin your diet. Then, compare the average to the electrical usage after you've been on a diet for a week. Consider encouraging everyone in your home to participate as well. You could also take your diet to your class and challenge the whole class to go on a diet. Finally, can you keep up the diet for two weeks? Three? A month? Calculate your energy savings.

Many internet resources can help you to calculate your carbon footprint or to identify ways to curb your energy use. The Environmental Protection Agency's Student's Guide to Global Climate Change has a
 calculator that is easy to use. **NASA's Climate Kids has additional information about what you can do to help the planet and its biodiversity.**

🔎 NASA climate kids help

GET TO KNOW YOUR FOOD

In the modern world, we often don't know or don't appreciate where our food comes from. But the food we eat may have a huge impact on the environment and biodiversity. To help protect biodiversity, you can make more informed food choices. For example, more than 75 percent of the ocean's fisheries are over-fished or depleted. When you eat seafood, choose food that is harvested or farmed sustainably.

> **Record what you eat for one week to get to know your food.** Determine where that food has come from. Could you eat more sustainably? What foods could be purchased from local farmers at farmers' markets or stores? Plan meals for one day that are more sustainable. Write your plan in your science journal.

> **Land-based food includes meat, fruits and vegetables, nuts, and more.** Even if you love eating meat, try cutting it out of your diet a day or two a week. This helps reduce carbon emissions because of the meat industry's carbon footprint.

> **When you do eat meat, try to find meat that is farmed locally and sustainably.** This supports your local farmers and reduces food miles (and thus carbon emissions!) at the same time. Sustainable farms also treat animals better and use fewer chemicals and pesticides.

> **Eat lots of vegetables!** Try to eat those that are locally produced. You can even grow your own!

Consider This

Was planning a more sustainable diet easier or more difficult than you thought? Was finding local meat and produce easy or is this difficult in your area? Can you challenge your family to go meatless every Monday? Try planning a week's worth of dinners that are more sustainable.

Cities and people around the world have joined the Meatless Monday movement for personal health and the health of the planet. **Visit the website for more information about the movement and for meatless recipes that are easy to make at home.**

🔍 meatless Monday

PLANT A BEE GARDEN

Many plants rely on bees and other insects for pollination to reproduce. Not only that, many of our crops depend on bees. Yet bees are at risk. Pesticides, habitat loss, monoculture farming, and disease are all threatening bee populations. You can help bees by creating a bee garden with a variety of plants that flower throughout the spring, summer, and fall.

❯ **The bee garden can be in a spot in your yard or in a large planter on a balcony or outside a window.** You could also talk to a ranger at your local park about planting bee-friendly flowers there. Research plants and bee species that are native to your area. In addition, find plants that flower at different times throughout the growing season.

❯ **Draw a plan for your garden.** You may even want to speak with an expert at your local garden store or farmers' market for more information. Then start planting!

❯ **How is your garden growing?** Are bees coming to it? Did you see bees in spring, summer, and fall? Evaluate your garden. What did you do right? Consider what you could do better next season. Perhaps enlist the help of friends or family to make your garden bigger.

DID YOU KNOW?

Honeybees are the only insects that produce food that humans eat. One bee makes approximately $\frac{1}{12}$ of a teaspoon of honey in its lifetime.

Consider This

Do you know any beekeepers? There are many people who keep bees as a hobby. Do some research online or ask at an agricultural organization to find out if there are any beekeepers in your town. Sometimes, there are beekeeping clubs that meet or offer informational days you could attend to learn more about bees and their importance to the environment.

Happy Earth Day!

Every April 22 is Earth Day around the world. It is a day to celebrate Earth, its ecosystems, and its biodiversity. It is also a day to bring awareness to the many issues affecting the health of the planet. The first Earth Day was celebrated on April 22, 1970, thanks to the efforts of a senator from Wisconsin named Gaylord Nelson (1916–2005), who saw a need to act to protect the planet. Earth Day is celebrated in communities around the world. You can be a part of it! Research events happening in your own community on the next Earth Day. Gather friends or family members and participate in an activity. Consider organizing your own event the next year. You might also challenge yourself, your friends, your family, and your classmates to consider every day Earth Day. What are simple things you could all do daily to help promote the health of our environment?

 Learn more about this growing environmental movement and the various efforts underway across the globe.

🔍 Earth Day

GLOSSARY

abiotic: of or relating to nonliving things such as temperature, wind, precipitation, soil type, and more.

acid rain: precipitation that has been polluted by acid.

adapt: to make changes to survive in new or different conditions.

adaptation: the changes a plant or animal has made to help it survive.

agriculture: growing plants and raising animals for food and other products.

algae: a simple organism found in water that is like a plant but without roots, stems, or leaves.

amphibian: an animal with moist skin that is born in water but lives on land. An amphibian changes its body temperature by moving to warmer or cooler places. Frogs, toads, newts, efts, and salamanders are amphibians.

anaerobic: able to live without oxygen.

ancestor: someone from your family who lived before you.

antibiotic: a medicine that can disable or kill bacteria.

antifreeze: a liquid that is added to a second liquid to lower the temperature at which the second liquid freezes.

ape: a large, tailless primate such as a gorilla, chimpanzee, or orangutan.

appendage: a part of an animal or plant that sticks out from the main part it is attached to, such as an arm or leg.

aquatic: related to water.

archaea: single-celled microbes that live in extremely harsh environments.

archaeological: having to do with archaeology, the study of ancient people through the objects they left behind.

arthropod: an invertebrate animal with a segmented body and limbs with joints, such as a spider or insect.

atmosphere: the mixture of gases that surround a planet.

bacteria: microorganisms found in soil, water, plants, and animals that are often beneficial but sometimes harmful.

behavioral: having to do with the way an organism acts and interacts with its environment and other organisms in order to survive.

biodiversity: diversity is a range of different things. Biodiversity is the variety of life on Earth.

biofuel: a fuel made from living matter, such as plants.

biogeography: the study of the distribution of biodiversity on Earth.

bioluminescent: when living things give off light by hosting a chemical reaction in their bodies.

biome: a large natural area with a distinctive climate, geology, set of water resources, and group of plants and animals that are adapted for life there.

biotic: of or relating to living things.

boll: the seed pod of the cotton plant that fluffy cotton fibers burst from.

boreal forest: a forest of coniferous trees found in the cold temperatures of the Northern Hemisphere.

camouflage: the colors or patterns that allow a plant or animal to blend in with its environment.

captive breeding: the process of mating wild animals to produce and raise offspring in places such as zoos, aquariums, reserves, and other conservation facilities.

carbon: an element that is found in all life on Earth and in coal, petroleum, and diamonds.

carbon dioxide (CO_2): a colorless, odorless gas. Humans and animals exhale this gas while plants absorb it—it is also a by-product of burning fossil fuels.

carbon footprint: the total amount of carbon dioxide and other greenhouse gases emitted over the full life cycle of a product or service, or by a person or family in a year.

carnivore: an animal that eats only other animals.

cell: the smallest unit, or building block, of an organism.

cellulose: a substance that is the main part of the cell walls of plants.

chemosynthesis: the process some organisms use to create energy from chemicals instead of the sun.

climate: average weather patterns in an area during a period of many years.

climate change: a change in long-term weather patterns, which happens through both natural and man-made processes.

collage: a work of art made up of different pieces of material.

conservation: managing and protecting natural resources.

consumer: an organism that eats other organisms.

convention: an agreement among countries.

coral bleaching: a sign of poor health in coral that happens when algae in the coral die or lose their color.

crops: plants grown for food and other uses.

crustacean: a group of marine animals that includes crabs, lobsters, shrimps, and barnacles.

cryptobiosis: a temporary state in which an organism's bodily process slows or stops under extreme conditions.

current: the steady flow of water or air in one direction.

cyanobacteria: a type of aquatic bacteria that produces oxygen through photosynthesis.

decompose: to rot or decay.

decomposer: an organism that breaks down organic matter.

deforestation: the process through which forests are cleared to use land for other purposes.

dehydrate: to take the water out of something.

DNA: the substance found in the cells of every living thing that determines everything about us, including whether we are human, an insect, or something else; have blue eyes or brown; are right- or left-handed; and every other trait that makes us who we are.

dormant: in a state of rest or inactivity.

drought: a long period of little or no rain.

Ebola: a disease caused by a virus that spreads easily; it causes severe internal bleeding and often death.

ecosystem: an interdependent community of living and nonliving things and their environment.

ecosystem diversity: the variety of ecosystems in a certain region.

ecosystem engineers: species that greatly alter an ecosystem by creating, modifying, maintaining, or destroying it.

ecosystem services: the important benefits provided by ecosystems to keep the earth's air, water, and soil healthy.

ecotourism: tourism designed to support conservation efforts.

ejecta: materials thrown out, as from the impact of an asteroid.

emission: something sent or given off, such as smoke, gas, heat, or light.

endemic: a plant or animal that is native to only a certain area.

epoch: a division of time within a period.

equator: an imaginary line around the earth, halfway between the North and South Poles.

era: a division of geologic time.

erosion: the gradual wearing away of the earth's surface, usually by water or wind.

estuary: a body of water where a river meets the ocean, with a mix of fresh water and salt water.

eukaryote: a class of organisms composed of one or more cells that contains a nucleus.

evolution: the process by which species change through time.

evolve: to gradually develop and change over time.

exoskeleton: a skeleton on the outside of a body.

extinction: the death of an entire species so that it no longer exists.

GLOSSARY

extremophile: an organism that thrives in environments that most other life forms cannot live in.

folklore: the traditional beliefs, customs, and stories of a community, passed through the generations by word of mouth.

food chain: a community of plants and animals where each is eaten by another higher up in the chain.

food miles: how far food travels from farm to table.

food security: having ongoing access to enough nutritious, affordable food.

food web: a network of connected food chains.

fossil fuel: natural fuel that formed long ago from the remains of living organisms. Oil, natural gas, and coal are fossil fuels.

fragmentation: the act of breaking something into smaller sections or pieces.

fungi: the plural of fungus, an organism that has no leaves, flowers, or roots and that lives on dead or rotting organic matter. Mushrooms are a fungus.

gene: instructions within cells that affect how an organism will look, grow, and act.

genetic diversity: the variety of genes within a species.

geography: the features of a place, such as mountains and rivers.

geologic time: the span of Earth's history marked by major events and changes.

global warming: an increase in the average temperature of the earth's atmosphere, enough to cause climate change.

gravity: the force that pulls objects together and holds you on Earth.

Great Oxygenation Event: the introduction of oxygen into the earth's atmosphere more than 2 billion years ago.

greenhouse effect: when the presence in the atmosphere of gases such as carbon dioxide, water vapor, and methane allow incoming sunlight to pass through, but then trap that heat.

habitat: a plant or animal's home, which supplies it with food, water, and shelter.

herbivore: an animal that eats only plants.

hydroelectric: energy from moving water converted to electricity.

hydrothermal vent: a fissure in the sea floor where super-heated fluid comes out.

infectious: illness that is spread by germs or viruses.

innovation: a new invention or way of doing something.

invasive species: a species that is not native to an ecosystem and rapidly expands to crowd out and harm other species.

invertebrate: an animal without a backbone.

kelp: a tall, brown seaweed that grows in forests in shallow ocean waters close to shore.

keystone species: a species that plays an essential role in an ecosystem, and without which the ecosystem would be greatly altered.

lichen: a plant-like organism made of algae and fungus that grows on solid surfaces such as rocks or trees.

malaria: a disease spread by infected mosquitoes. It is found mainly in the hot areas near the equator.

mammal: an animal that has a constant body temperature and is mostly covered with hair or fur. Humans, dogs, horses, and mice are mammals.

mass extinction: a period in the earth's history when very large numbers of species die out in a short period of time.

medicinal: having properties that can be used to treat illnesses.

megafauna: very large animals.

microbe: a tiny living or nonliving thing.

microbiome: a community of microbes.

microorganism: a living thing so small that it can be seen only with a microscope.

microplastic: a tiny piece of plastic less than 0.2 inch in size.

GLOSSARY

mineral: a naturally occurring solid found in rocks and in the ground.

molten: turned into liquid through heat.

monoculture: the farming of a single crop or animal in one area.

mycorrhizal fungi: fungi that grow on the roots of plants to provide them with water and nutrients. These fungi also receive nutrients from the plants they grow on.

nanofiber: a very thin strand of material.

native: a species that naturally belongs in an ecosystem.

natural selection: one of the basic means of evolution in which organisms that are well-adapted to their environment are better able to survive, reproduce, and pass along their useful traits to offspring.

neuron: a special cell that sends electrical and chemical messages to your brain.

nutrients: substances in food and soil that living things need to live and grow.

ocean acidification: the process by which the ocean absorbs carbon dioxide from the atmosphere, and through a series of chemical reactions, becomes more acidic.

organic matter: decaying plants and animals.

organism: a living plant, animal, or single-celled form of life.

over-exploitation: the hunting or taking of a natural resource (such as animals or trees) faster than the population can reproduce, which often leads to extinction.

period: a division of geologic time within an era.

permafrost: permanently frozen subsoil and rock just beneath the surface of the ground.

pesticide: a chemical used to kill pests such as rodents or insects.

photosynthesis: the process plants use to turn sunlight, carbon dioxide, and water into food.

physical: relating to the body.

phytoplankton: microscopic plants at the base of the marine food web.

poaching: the illegal hunting and killing of animals.

polar regions: the areas of the earth around the North and South Poles, within the Arctic and Antarctic Circles.

pollinate: to transfer pollen from the male parts of flowers to the female parts so that flowers can make seeds. Pollen is a powder made by flowers that is needed for the flower to make a seed.

precipitation: the falling to Earth of rain, snow, or any form of water.

predator: an animal or plant that kills and eats another animal.

prey: to hunt. Also animals hunted by other animals.

primate: any member of a group of animals that includes humans, apes, and monkeys.

producer: a part of a food chain that includes all plants that make their own food through photosynthesis.

refuge: a place that provides protection or safety.

renewable energy: power that comes from sources that will never run out, such as the sun and wind.

reptile: an animal covered with scales that crawls on its belly or on short legs. A reptile changes its body temperature by moving to warmer or cooler places. Snakes, turtles, lizards, alligators, and crocodiles are reptiles.

resource: anything people use to take care of themselves, such as water, food, and building materials.

runoff: produced when water picks up wastes as it flows over the surface of the ground. Runoff can pollute streams, lakes, rivers, and oceans.

salinity: the amount of salt in water.

SARS: Severe Acute Respiratory Syndrome, a serious disease caused by a virus that spreads easily; it affects the lungs and breathing and can cause death.

savanna: a dry, rolling grassland with scattered shrubs and trees.

sediment: material deposited by water, wind, or glaciers.

sedimentation: the process of solid matter settling to the bottom of water.

single-use: describes an item that is made to be used only one time and then thrown away.

species: a group of living things that are closely related and can produce offspring.

species diversity: the variety of species living in an area.

spore: a structure produced by fungi that sprouts and grows into a new fungus.

sustainable: designed to minimize environmental impact.

temperate zone: the area of the earth that lies between the tropics and the polar regions.

terrestrial: related to land.

theory of evolution: a scientific theory that explains how species change through time and how all species have evolved from simple life forms.

toxic: poisonous.

treaty: a formal agreement between two or more countries.

trilobite: an ancient arthropod that lived during the Paleozoic era.

tropical zone: the area of the earth around the equator.

tsunami: an enormous wave formed by a disturbance under the water, such as an earthquake or volcano.

tundra: a treeless Arctic region that is permanently frozen below the top layer of soil.

turbine: a machine with blades turned by the force of water, air, or steam.

United Nations (UN): an international organization created to promote peace and cooperation among nations.

variations: the behavioral and physical differences among members of a species.

vertebrate: an organism with a backbone or spinal column.

wastewater: dirty water that has been used by people in their homes, in factories, and in other businesses.

watershed: the land area that drains into a river or a lake.

wetlands: low areas filled with water, such as a marsh or swamp.

Metric Conversions

Use this chart to find the metric equivalents to the English measurements in this book. If you need to know a half measurement, divide by two. If you need to know twice the measurement, multiply by two. How do you find a quarter measurement? How do you find three times the measurement?

English	Metric
1 inch	2.5 centimeters
1 foot	30.5 centimeters
1 yard	0.9 meter
1 mile	1.6 kilometers
1 pound	0.5 kilogram
1 teaspoon	5 milliliters
1 tablespoon	15 milliliters
1 cup	237 milliliters

RESOURCES

MOVIE

Planet Earth. Alastair Fothergill, Series Producer. BBC, 2006. 5 DVD set.

BOOKS

Burillo-Kirch, Christine. *Microbes: Discover an Unseen World with 25 Projects*. Nomad Press, 2015.

Castaldo, Nancy. *The Story of Seeds*. HMH Books for Young Readers, 2016.

Sartore, Joel. *National Geographic The Photo Ark: One Man's Quest to Document the World's Animals*. National Geographic, 2017.

Sharma, Richa. *Green Genius Guide: What are Ecosystems, Biomes, Ecotones, and more...* The Energy and Resources Institute, 2013 (reprint).

WEBSITES

A Bee is More Than a Bug: *climatekids.nasa.gov/bees*

Biodiversity Web Video: *youtube.com/watch?v=HA3xNMJnFuo*

A Brief History of Life, NOVA: *pbs.org/wgbh/nova/evolution/brief-history-life.html*

Center for Biological Diversity: *biologicaldiversity.org/about/story*

Global Youth Biodiversity Network: *gybn.org/about-2/what-is-gybn*

Nature NOW: *pbs.org/wnet/nature/blog*

Ocean, The Smithsonian Institution: *www.si.edu*

QR CODE GLOSSARY

page 2: *video.nationalgeographic.com/video/magazine/ my-shot-minute/ngm-biodiversity-msm?source=relatedvideo*

page 20: *becominghuman.org/node/interactive-documentary*

page 21: *hhmi.org/biointeractive/deep-history-life-earth*

page 23: *onezoom.org*

page 25: *cdn.makezine.com/make/wp_aquanaut.pdf*

page 34: *marine-conservation.org/media/shining_sea/s2ss_globe.htm*

page 37: *video.nationalgeographic.com/video/short-film-showcase/ explore-the-hidden-and-fragile-world-inside-caves*

page 39: *ocean.si.edu/ocean-videos/organisms-beneath-sand*

RESOURCES

ESSENTIAL QUESTIONS

Introduction: How is everything on the planet related to everything else?

Chapter 1: How has life on Earth become so diverse?

Chapter 2: Where is biodiversity found?

Chapter 3: Why is biodiversity so important?

Chapter 4: How is biodiversity important to humans?

Chapter 5: What are the threats to biodiversity today?

Chapter 6: What can we do to protect biodiversity on Earth?

INDEX

INDEX